Managing Image Collections

DATE DUE

			Printed in USA

CHANDOS
INFORMATION PROFESSIONAL SERIES

Series Editor: Ruth Rikowski
(email: Rikowskigr@aol.com)

Chandos' new series of books are aimed at the busy information professional. They have been specially commissioned to provide the reader with an authoritative view of current thinking. They are designed to provide easy-to-read and (most importantly) practical coverage of topics that are of interest to librarians and other information professionals. If you would like a full listing of current and forthcoming titles, please visit our web site www.chandospublishing.com or email info@chandospublishing.com or telephone +44 (0) 1223 891358.

New authors: we are always pleased to receive ideas for new titles; if you would like to write a book for Chandos, please contact Dr Glyn Jones on email gjones@chandospublishing.com or telephone number +44 (0) 1993 848726.

Bulk orders: some organisations buy a number of copies of our books. If you are interested in doing this, we would be pleased to discuss a discount. Please email info@chandospublishing.com or telephone +44 (0) 1223 891358.

Managing Image Collections

A practical guide

MARGOT NOTE

Chandos Publishing
TBAC Business Centre
Avenue 4
Station Lane
Witney
Oxford OX28 4BN
UK
Tel: +44 (0) 1993 848726
Email: info@chandospublishing.com
www.chandospublishing.com

Chandos Publishing is an imprint of Woodhead Publishing Limited

Woodhead Publishing Limited
80 High Street
Sawston, Cambridge CB22 3HJ
UK
Tel: +44 (0) 1223 499140
Fax: +44 (0) 1223 832819
www.woodheadpublishing.com

First published in 2011

ISBN:

978 1 84334 599 2

© M. Note, 2011

British Library Cataloguing-in-Publication Data.
A catalogue record for this book is available from the British Library.

Typeset by Domex e-Data Pvt. Ltd.
Printed in the UK and USA.

This book is dedicated to Margaret Cross Norton
and other female cultural heritage leaders
who blazed the trail for women like me.

Contents

List of figures, tables, and boxes

Figures

Tables

Boxes

Acknowledgments

During the writing of this book, many individuals and institutions provided help, advice, and inspiration, and it is impossible to name all to whom I owe a debt of gratitude. However, from that number, I would like to thank the following: above all else, my partner, Bill Florio, for his support and feedback; my family, Charles and Pamela Note, Martin Note, 'Big' Bill and Irene Florio, Mike and Lorraine McInerney, David and Jo-Ann Leis, Antoinette DeNigris, and Betty Germano; Mary Lynn Ventola for generously providing historical images; the iSchool faculty at Drexel University, notably Susan Davis, Bob Allen, and Mike Miller, as my course work formed the cornerstone of this book; Max Marmor of the Kress Foundation; and Bonnie Burnham, Lisa Ackerman, and my colleagues at the World Monuments Fund. Special thanks to the Society of American Archivists, Indiana University Student Chapter, for inviting me to present on image management at their 2010 conference.

About the author

Margot Note has spent her career working in the cultural heritage sector, including in small liberal arts colleges, public and academic libraries, and archives. Beyond her involvement in all aspects of historic photographic collections, her research interests include user-centered design, planning and managing the delivery of digital cultural information, improving access to primary sources, and information-seeking behavior. She has published reviews on many aspects of archival science, information management, and library services in *American Archivist, College & Research Libraries, Journal of Academic Librarianship,* and *Libraries & the Cultural Record*, among other publications. She holds a Master's in History from Sarah Lawrence College, a Master's in Library and Information Science, and a Post-Master's Certificate in Archives and Records Management, both from Drexel University. She is a Certified Archivist based in New York and is the Director of Archives and Information Management at the World Monuments Fund, an international historic preservation organization.

The author can be contacted via the publisher.

Introduction

The soul never thinks without an image. (Aristotle)

Everything transitory is but an image. (Johann Wolfgang von Goethe)

Photography concentrates one's eye on the superficial. For that reason it obscures the hidden life which glimmers through the outlines of things like a play of light and shade. One can't catch that even with the sharpest lens. One has to grope for it by feeling. (Franz Kafka, 1921)

Since the first drawings in the caves at Lascaux, France were executed almost twenty-two thousand years ago, information has been shared via evolving systems of pictures and symbols. Cave paintings and online image collections are both 'digital', the former created by drawing the fingers across clay, the latter created by computer manipulation. Greisdorf and O'Connor (2008) assert, "We are at once linked from twenty-first-century digital images to the digital images of our ancestors, reminded that the computer-based use of the term is anchored in our very physical nature and reminded that construction of images is a purposeful act" (6). From their earliest existence, humans have striven to create, replicate, and disseminate visual information. As Taylor (1979) notes, "The first statements to survive the sound of a voice were pictures, not words" (418). Even the First Commandment warned not against murder, adultery, or theft, but against the making of graven images.

L'Heliographie

Sometime between June 4 and July 18, 1827, the first permanent photograph was created. *View from the Window at Le Gras* was the work of Frenchman Joseph Nicéphore Niépce (1765–1833). The image was taken from the second floor of his family home, Le Gras, in the village of Saint-Loup-de-Varennes, less than three miles from the village of Chalon-sur-Saône in Burgundy. It was made using a polished pewter plate coated with a solution of bitumen of Judea, an asphalt derivative of petroleum, and exposed for over eight hours in a camera with a biconvex lens, to create a latent image. It was then washed with a solvent of oil of lavender and white petroleum to dissolve the areas of bitumen that had not been hardened by the light. The highlights of the image were made from the hardened bitumen, while the darker areas were the pewter plate itself. The result was a direct positive, latterly reversed picture. Niépce called it a *heliograph* or 'sun drawing,' a word that "conjur[ed] a long lineage of theological and classical associations" (Batchen 1999, 63).

His correspondence reveals that he had been trying to make similar images since 1816 (Batchen 1999). He was interested in the newly invented art of lithography, introduced into France in 1802 with the establishment of the premier lithographic studio in Paris in 1813. Lithography, the first fundamentally new printing technology since the invention of relief printing in the fifteenth century, is a technique for reproducing images that is based on the chemical repellence of oil and water. After experimenting with paper, glass, and stone surfaces and resins that hardened when exposed to light, he began using pewter plates in 1826.

In early June 1827, Niépce wrote to his fellow countryman Louis-Jacques-Mandé Daguerre (1787–1851), the inventor of the daguerreotype, that he would continue his photographic experiments: "I shall take them up again today because the countryside is in the full splendor of its attire and I shall devote myself exclusively to the copying of views from nature" (Gernsheim and Gernsheim 1968, 56–57). The image he produced shortly afterward shows, from left to right, a dovecote (or pigeon house), a pear tree with sky showing through its branches, a slanted barn roof, a recessed baking kitchen, and another wing of the house. Because of the sun's movement during the eight hours that the picture was exposed, the sunlight appears to be shining on the roof and both ends of the buildings.

The view was familiar to him as he gazed through his study window over the courtyard, and the location allowed a day-long exposure without interruption. He used this view in his experiments with different chemical and material components and compared the results for over a decade. For instance, on May 5, 1815, Niépce wrote to his brother Claude, "I saw on the white paper all that part of the birdhouse that is seen from the window and a faint image of the casement, which was less illuminated than the exterior objects" (Potonniée 1973, 82).

After traveling to London to visit Claude in 1827, Niépce sought financial support from the Royal Society, but was unsuccessful because he would not reveal the details of his photographic technique. Before returning to France in February 1828, he left the image with his host, Francis Bauer, a British botanist and botanical artist. Bauer wrote on the paper backing of the frame:

> *L'Heliographie.*
> *Les premiers résultats*
> *obtenus Spontanément*
> *par l'action de la lumiere.*
> *Par Monsieur Niepce*
> *De Chalon sur Saone.*
> *1827.*
>
> *Monsieur Niépce's first successful*
> *experiment of fixing permanently*
> *the Image from Nature.*

Bauer signed his name and his address, Kew Green, at the bottom. After returning to France, Niépce, who was a life-long inventor, continued his experiments.

Over fifty years later, photography historian Helmut Gernsheim (1913–1995) traced the work's history, and discovered the photograph on February 15, 1952 in a trunk in England, where it had been forgotten. Gernsheim (1977) wrote, "Only a historian can understand my feeling at that moment. I had reached the goal of my research and held the foundation stone of photography in my hand."

When discovered, the image, though permanent, was so faint that it looked like a mirror. After attempts by the Research Laboratory of the Eastman Kodak Company to reproduce the photograph, Gernsheim used watercolor on a gelatin silver print to mimic how he thought it must have originally appeared. His retouched version, not the Kodak reproduction, is the most often replicated image in photographic histories. Batchen (1999) notes:

> Here we have another one of those peculiar twists of photographic history. The image that is everywhere propagated as the first photograph, as the foundation stone of photography's history, as the origin of the medium, is in fact a painting after a drawing! The much touted first photograph turns out to be a representation of a representation and therefore, according to photo-history's own definition, not a photograph at all. We have instead a painted

> version of a reproduction that itself [in Gernsheim's words] "in no way corresponded with the original." It seems that wherever we look for photography's bottom line, we face this strange economy of deferral, an origin always preceded by another, more original, but never-quite-present photographic instance. (127)

Photography historians have argued as much about the first photograph as they have about the first photographer. The birth of photography remains elusive, but surviving images enable us to determine a starting point for the history of the medium. Historians may dispute photography's beginnings, but all scholars know Niépce's image. Gernsheim (1982) calls it "the world's earliest, and the inventor's sole surviving photograph from nature" (34). Batchen (1999) concurs, writing that the image is an "undisputed icon" (125).

Viewing the first photograph

In the midst of researching and writing this book, I visited my brother in Austin, Texas for the winter holidays. It was kismet that the First Photograph, as it is called, is housed at the Harry Ransom Center on the local University of Texas campus. In 1963, Gernsheim donated the heliograph to Harry Huntt Ransom, the university's vice president and provost, when he purchased his photography collection.

I had viewed the image online and in publications, both the original and retouched reproductions. As a director of a digitization initiative in my organization, I was a believer in the power and accessibility of digital images, yet, trained as a historian and archivist, I also valued the physicality of artifacts. Viewing the heliograph was an opportunity to gauge if the analog experience would provide more information to me as a researcher, or if studying the digital version alone was adequate.

The exhibit was situated in a glass-enclosed lobby, but ingeniously constructed to look as if the viewer was entering the photograph's casing; Bauer's note in his graceful handwriting was on the outside. The heliograph was enclosed in its original presentational frame, under controlled lighting to make the image visible. In the darkened space, my heart beat wildly. It was as if I were Gernsheim, discovering the image emerging from its mirrored surface. The picture looked like an archeological remnant, yet, at the same time, its jumble of shapes resembled an abstract painting.

Figure I.1 View from the Window at Le Gras, by Joseph Nicéphore Niépce, c. 1826

Note: This image, the first successful permanent photograph, is the genesis of the process of photography which has had a transforming influence on the world for more than 150 years. Although Gernsheim's 1952 image is more well-known among scholars, this image, taken in 2002 by the Getty Conservation Institute, is the more accurate reproduction of the artifact.

Source: Heliotype, recto, 10.2 x 11.4 in (25.8 x 29 cm). Gernsheim Collection, Harry Ransom Humanities Research Center, University of Texas at Austin.

Viewing the analog original and digital reproduction provided complementary experiences. I had studied *View from the Window at Le Gras* most thoroughly on my own, but the materialization of the image in its physical form provided me with a deeper appreciation of it, a new way of seeing the image in both its analog and digital forms, and an understanding of the value of both for researchers.

Images defined

To define 'image' in its complex historical, philosophical, and linguistic context deserves encyclopedic treatment. 'Image,' for the purposes of this book, is defined in its most literal manner: a representational picture or "any predominantly two-dimensional static item or items that convey information in the form of images" (Shatford 1984, 13). An image is a "graphic, pictorial representation: a concrete material object," even if that physical manifestation is a digital file, and a "non-moving representation of visual information" (Mitchell 1984, 504; Anderson et al. 2006, 7). 'Image' connotes the idea of purposeful construction and composition of the content, no matter what the medium.

Visual formats include photographs, drawings, paintings, slides, prints, posters, and architectural and cartographic records. Visual materials are synonymous with 'nontextual records,' which "include records formats that are not principally words on paper, such as maps, photographs, motion pictures and video, sound recordings, and the like" and 'nonprint materials' which are "items that are not books, periodicals, or pamphlets; nonbook materials" (Pearce-Moses 2005). Library and archival science literature sometimes refers to images as 'nontextual' or 'graphic' material or 'special media,' but Schwartz (2002) notes that this terminology marginalizes them, performing a linguistic 'othering' of visual materials against the textual-format norm. Coming to terms with photographs, so to speak, requires uncomplicated language that expresses how visual formats are their own, equitable subject of study. Thus, 'images,' 'visual materials,' 'pictures,' and 'photographs' will be used interchangeably throughout this book. Photographs are the focus of the book because they are the predominant visual medium in archives and libraries. These institutions evaluate images' enduring values for research, rather than from the primary aesthetic, fine-art viewpoints of the museum.

The term 'photography', derived from the Greek words for 'light' and 'draw,' refers to a number of processes, most of which were designed to produce images by means of chemical changes initiated by light. No matter what the technique needed to create them, photographs share a common structure. Photographs are formed by an image obtained through light being projected onto a base material, which can be glass, paper, or film, which has been coated with a light-sensitive material in the form of an emulsion, usually albumin or gelatin with silver halide salts to make black and white images, or pigments and dyes to form color images. The image is then developed and fixed using various chemicals.

At its most basic level, a photograph is a picture, likeness, or facsimile obtained by photography. Throughout its history, the definition has covered daguerreotypes, albumen prints, Polaroids, and various digital processes. These differences recall the inherent complexity and shifting nature of what constitutes a photograph.

There has been no single, coherent physical object that one can call a photograph, and the very term is a convenient catch-all for a wide array of pictures on paper, metal, glass, fabric, canvas and so forth whose only common quality is the involvement of light and chemistry at some point in the generative process. (McCauley 1997, 87)

The meaning of a photograph, its efficacy as an image, and its value as an object will always be dependent on the contexts within which it is read.

The earliest photographic prints were generated by printing-out processes. With this technique, sensitized paper was exposed to light beneath a negative and allowed to darken until an image appeared, without further chemical treatment. In contrast, developing-out processes, formed by chemically treating exposed sensitized paper, were not widely favored until the end of the nineteenth century. The natural tint of a photographic image is dependent on the number and size of the silver particles that make up the image. Printing out produces a comparatively low number of particles, which appear brownish. The image formed by chemical development consists of a greater number of larger silver particles that appear more neutral in color and denser in tone. A photograph which is printed on paper usually requires a negative, made of either glass or, since the twentieth century, flexible film, whereas a transparency or slide is a positive image and requires no negative, but needs light to be projected through the image for it to become visible.

Collections defined

'Collection,' as used in this book, relates to any discrete group of materials with some unifying characteristic that are organized systematically. "*Collection* refers to any groupings of photographs that include formal record groups, series, family papers, corporate records, and thematically assembled collections—sometimes called artificial collections" (Ritzenthaler and Vogt-O'Connor 2006, xv). Collections usually contain not only resources, but also additional information that may assist in their use, such as finding aids or metadata.

A thorough definition of digital collections is provided in *A Framework of Guidance for Building Good Digital Collections* (NISO 2007). The Framework identifies seven principles that apply to good digital collections. They should have an explicit collection development policy; be described so that users can discover their scope, restrictions on access, and other characteristics easily; be sustainable over time; be usable by as wide a variety of people as possible; respect intellectual property rights; have mechanisms to record information demonstrating how the collection is being used; and fit into larger initiatives.

The book stresses practices for organizing, preserving, and accessing collections, not individual images. Working with groups of related materials allows information professionals to highlight relationships among them and has value to researchers. Institutions can obtain the greatest management benefit for the smallest expenditure of resources and staff time when they address the needs of collections, as this ensures a level of control over many photographs, rather than a few.

Objectives

Managing Image Collections: A practical guide places photographic processes in a historical and contextual framework. The book's focus is on photographs that have enduring documentary value as resource materials for research, publication, exhibition, and teaching, rather than as fine art. It is intended to be a reference for institutions that choose to convert cultural resources into digital formats, while still maintaining hybrid collections of analog and digital images.

'Hybrid' is the key word here, defined as something having two kinds of components that produce the same or similar results. Photography, at its most basic level, is a technique for absorbing the energy of light into a recording medium and transforming it to create an image. In film, the light energy causes a chemical change in the silver halide crystals. In digital sensors, absorbed light is transformed into electricity. Beyond these actions, however, there are few similarities between analog and digital images. As photography moves from the realm of the physical to the realm of the electronic circuit, information professionals are responsible for managing, making accessible, and preserving analog and digital images in a cohesive manner, despite their formats' different characteristics.

The book advocates an integrated approach to digital initiatives, from selection, to access, to preservation, with an emphasis on the intersection of cultural objectives and practical digital applications. Readers will gain the knowledge to manage the digitization process from beginning to end, assess and define the needs of their particular project, and evaluate digitization options.

While photographs are used increasingly to support a broad range of research topics, their management remains far from standardized. Since every institution and image collection is different, the book does not prescribe specific technologies, procedures, or metadata schemes. Additionally, an unavoidable risk when writing about technology is that references to products, computer hardware specifications, current standards, and other similar details can quickly become outdated. As with the images themselves, image management begins with an understanding of context. There is no right way to manage images; there are only best practices that inform decisions based on the reasons for digitizing, the nature of the images, the institutional mission, available resources, the technical infrastructure, and user requirements.

Although this book is called a practical guide, a theoretical understanding of the challenges of images is required; the one is simply not possible without the other. The aim of the book is to provide a useful balance between theory and practice so as to assist readers to select strategies which best meet the current and projected future needs of their institutions.

While the book aims to be as comprehensive as possible, when it comes to image collections and the ways in which they expand and challenge informational practice, the coverage has had to be selective. Certain topics are covered in a cursory fashion, although they could easily be the subjects of entire books. The contents of *Managing Image Collections: A practical guide* should be viewed as the chief areas within a larger territory of inquiry.

Three appendices provide additional pertinent information. Appendix A: Digital project considerations presents a series of questions, an *aide-mémoire* to be explored before commencing a digitization initiative. Appendix B: Glossary of image collection terms provides definitions of terminology used in the management of analog, digitized, and born-digital image collections. Appendix C: Further reading lists print and online sources for specific topics that may interest readers. URLs are current as of November, 2010.

Images and figures

In order to keep the size and price of the book within reason, I have used far fewer photographs than is desirable in a book about images. In

Camera Lucida (1981), Roland Barthes wrote about finding a picture of his mother after her death to bring her back to life for a moment. Taken in 1898, the image shows her at five years old, standing in a winter garden and "holding one finger in the other hand, as children often do, in an awkward gesture" (69). Here, he writes, he had "at last rediscovered my mother" (70). Despite his attempts to put the image into words, the experience itself is so unique to him that he sees no point in reproducing the photograph in the book. While I am no Roland Barthes, I have selected a few historical photographs to illustrate points when necessary, with the knowledge that no number of images can truly explicate photography's complexity. Readers should consult photographs—owned by their institutions and others—in order to pursue visual analysis. My hope is that they will substitute their own image collections for my examples and correlate the information presented here to their own needs.

The book also contains figures, flowcharts, and suggestions for best practices in order to elaborate upon issues raised in the text, as well as to serve as a ready reference for future use.

Audience

The book is intended primarily for library, archives, and museum professionals. Additionally, students in these fields are introduced to the concept of digitizing collections and creating surrogates of cultural heritage materials that will be valuable resources well into the future.

Throughout this book, I use the phrase 'information professionals' rather than the more specific 'archivists,' 'librarians,' or 'curators.' This is done in part because the management of images for research affects diverse institutions. Historical photography collections are held in academic research libraries, historical societies, natural history collections, special collections libraries, commercial archives, and local, municipal, state, and federal records offices. Many collections of cultural heritage images lie well outside the purview of research institutions, and special efforts are required to identify and properly preserve these materials.

Those with responsibilities for managing images are not necessarily archivists, librarians, or curators; they can be information managers, conservators, specialists, technicians, and a plethora of other titles. They can also be full- or part-time employees, interns, or volunteers. Additionally, with hybrid collections, boundaries are disappearing, as the delivery of electronic resources involves stakeholders from many departments: faculty, information technologists, academic administrators, and others. Although archives, libraries, and museums have greatly contributed to the field, no single type of institution has the ultimate answer to the challenges of image management.

Information professionals, as defined in this book, are people who use information strategically to advance the mission of their organization through the development, deployment, and management of information resources and services. The usage of this term is meant to be inclusive of all those who are responsible for the administration of images for research purposes.

Why *Managing Image Collections: A practical guide*?

This book offers a different perspective than other books on similar subjects by concentrating solely on the management of analog, digitized, and born-digital images. Current books on managing digital imaging projects abound, as well as older texts on the preservation and access of analog image collections. This book blends the two, and assumes that while guidelines for managing analog image collections have already been established within the institution, digitization initiatives and the management of digital images may be new endeavors. As Ester (1996) notes:

> Digital images are beginning to stack up like cordwood as museums and archives plunge into more and more electronic application. Yet from a management standpoint, it is not at all clear that collections of digital files are any easier to manage than collections of film and prints. At least with photographic materials, institutions have had decades to develop filing and recording methods. (18)

Books on information management often focus too specifically on an institution type (such as archives, libraries, or museums) or on formats (either print and paper-based collections, still images, moving images, recorded sound, or broadcast media, or, in some cases, all of these). Often, the assumption is that the institution is large, has many staff members dedicated to image management, or has enough funding for large-scale projects.

Some manuals are very technical without first explaining the fundamentals, which can be overwhelming to those new to digital imaging. Other books focus on case studies and, while information professionals can learn from these experiences, it may be difficult to translate the lessons learned at one institution into the practices of another.

The book has been written for those faced with the task of preserving and making accessible historical image collections with limited staff, resources, and familiarity with the subject. Through work experience, graduate education, professional development opportunities, extensive research, and writing this book, I have gained knowledge about a topic that I am passionate about, and I have striven to create the book that I wish I had had when I began my career.

Other resources

Since image management is a rapidly changing field, with new technological developments and professional responses, this book does not stand alone and should be regarded as providing a gateway to further information on the subjects it covers. Readers are encouraged to peruse the following well-regarded books.

A. R. Kenney and O. Y. Rieger's (2000) *Moving Theory into Practice: Digital imaging for libraries and archives* provides an excellent overview of imaging projects and the issues that confront those implementing them, featuring the opinions of many experts in the field, giving short, in-depth, and balanced coverage of many relevant issues. Selection strategies, digital image creation, quality control, image management, metadata, rights management, access control, and preservation are among the topics covered. Each chapter includes sidebar reviews of important aspects of digitization.

S. D. Lee's (2001) *Digital Imaging: A practical handbook* deals with managerial issues in undertaking digitization, such as selection criteria, implementing the digitization workflow, and funding opportunities. The book provides flowcharts and worksheets for decision making and budget preparation. These are extremely useful in beginning a digital imaging project, particularly if the institution has no previous experience with digitization. Careful attention is also paid to cataloging, metadata, delivery systems, copyright, and image protection.

L. Hughes's (2004) *Digitizing Collections: Strategic issues for the information manager* details both practical and strategic issues that need to be understood before making material available online, such as the advantages and drawbacks of digitization and developing institutional procedures and strategies. Topics include selection management, intellectual property and copyright, project management, technology standards, metadata, and handling and digitizing rare and fragile items.

L. MacDonald's (2006) edited volume *Digital Heritage: Applying digital imaging to cultural heritage* contains chapters written by those using digital imaging to document and conserve cultural heritage assets and to produce higher-quality records and better analytical tools for condition assessment. All the contributors stress issues of usability, presenting a historical and holistic view of the evolving nature of user requirements for digital projects.

M. Ritzenthaler and D. Vogt-O'Connor's (2006) *Photographs: Archival care and management* explains how to best preserve and use photographs with historical value. All aspects of photograph management are covered, from appraisal and accessioning through digital conversion and reference. Its focus is on the development of systems to organize, preserve, and access collections.

1

Photographic image history

Abstract: Comprehending the history of photography provides an intellectual foundation for information professionals working in cultural heritage institutions to preserve a vast and challenging photographic legacy. Additionally, knowledge of photographic formats in historic collections is an integral part of a comprehensive understanding of the complex medium of photography. Focusing on photographs with enduring value as resources for research, publication, exhibition, and teaching, this chapter explores the development of photographic records from historical, aesthetic, and sociological perspectives. Photography's history reveals the range of different materials, chemicals, and processes involved in capturing images, as well as the technical developments of plates, film, and cameras. Photography's commercial expansion, the development of image collections, color photography, and digital technology are also explored.

Keywords: *cartes-de-visite*, daguerreotypes, digital technology, image collections, photographic history

> The very things which an artist would leave out, or render imperfectly, the photograph takes infinite care with, and so renders its illusions perfect. What is the picture of a drum without the marks on its head where the beating of the sticks has darkened the parchment? (Oliver Wendell Holmes, 1859)

> A knowledge of photography is just as important as that of the alphabet. The illiterate of the future will be ignorant of the use of camera and pen alike. (László Moholy-Nagy, 1923)

> Photography can never grow up if it imitates some other medium. It has to walk alone; it has to be itself. (Berenice Abbott)

Introduction

At the end of the twentieth century, digital images emerged as the dominant visual medium. "The means by which we create and share image information is rapidly changing, as digital photography stands poised to replace its film-based predecessor" (Terras 2008, viii). The ease of which digital images can be taken, manipulated, and distributed supports the claim that digital photography has already replaced analog image capturing. For instance, in 2007, over 90 percent of cameras sold were digital, nearly a billion camera phones were in use, and an estimated 250 billion digital photos were taken (Ritchen 2008, 11). Digital photographs blur the traditional definition of photography because images are made by means of a photoelectric effect. Some historians believe that digital technology embodies a continuation of themes and practices associated with chemical photography, but others suggest that digital images are radically different from what preceded them. When it was introduced in the nineteenth century, photography threatened painting, as its mechanical technique became more popular and affordable than the handmade arts. In the twenty-first century, digital photography may result in an even more distant relationship to analog photography. Digital photography expresses a monumental change while, paradoxically, citing a medium that dates from the industrial era.

Although digital photography shares a similar developmental pattern with the early history of traditional photography, which was grounded in scientific inquiry and discovery, a more critical examination reveals that digital images possess some fundamentally new and different technical properties. The new production and distribution practices of digital imagery are radically changing the ways in which images are used, understood, and valued. For instance, digital imaging technology began to permeate the communications industry by the 1980s. Enthusiasm for the possibilities of this new medium gave way to concern, as digital images can be altered in innumerable ways. The emergence of digital technology, which allows for the manipulation of images without leaving any evidence of the intervention, poses a fundamental challenge to traditional notions of documentary evidence.

Additionally, while traditional photography is losing its influence in photojournalism and amateur photography, the analog photograph is increasingly becoming an object of public discourse. In the past few decades, historians and other scholars in the humanities have widened their interests. It would have been impossible to conduct research in relatively new fields in the humanities—such as women's history, labor history, material culture, etc.—if scholars had limited themselves to the traditional records of evidential value preserved in archives. Images, specifically photographs, are part of this broader range of evidence. In the mid 1960s, Raphael Samuel and other historians became aware of the value of photographs as evidence for nineteenth-century social history, helping them to construct a 'history from below' focusing on the everyday life and experiences of ordinary people. In 1985, a symposium on the evidence of art was held by American historians, published in a special issue of the *Journal of Interdisciplinary History*. The subject attracted so much interest that it was soon republished as a book, *Art and History: Images and their meanings* (1988). Since then, images have increasingly been used by:

> historians, teachers and students, illustrators, architects, designers and hobbyists, collectors and curators of various objects, even by librarians. Everyone accepts that the art historian needs pictures to pursue his or her research, but other kinds of historians find information in photographs and drawings, in paintings and prints, useful for their study of the past. (Shatford 1986, 41)

Images are now treated as evidence in and of themselves, not supplemental to text, but records in their own right.

Information professionals working in archives, libraries, museums, and similar institutions find themselves dealing with visual collections that are in transition, shifting from chemically processed to digitally produced materials. Images "can be very intimidating to the non-specialist who is forced to deal with them simply because his institution owns them and there is no photography specialist" (Dooley 1995, 85). Images "prompt complex rhetorical negotiations," are "fertile, underused and vulnerable to misinterpretation," and "have not received the level of intellectual research needed to develop the theoretical bases behind their access" (Finnegan 2006, 121; Mifflin 2007, 32; Beaudoin 2007, 24).

The principles underlying the management of digital images are the same as those that support analog collections. Their practical application may differ according to the needs of one medium or the other, but where records in both media are to be managed in tandem, there is a need for as much commonality as can be achieved in this hybrid environment. "Recognition of the significance of photographs depends upon an understanding of the historical developments depicted in the images and of photographic technologies, aesthetics, and attitudes" (Huyda 1977, 10). Knowledge of photographic processes can assist in identification and interpretation, preservation and storage, and digitization, as well as in a plethora of other image collection-related activities. Image collections:

have not enjoyed a high profile in libraries and archives, and although recognized by users as extremely valuable, have not generally been the object of the serious consideration of [information professionals], [but] the reality of the contemporary information economy is that images are in higher circulation and higher demand than words and print. (Turner 1993, 245; Harris 2006, 213)

Technology and images

Photographic technology did not develop linearly, one process replacing another, but with a number of processes used concurrently for their aesthetic or economic values. Each medium filters the world according to its own characteristics. "By the last half of the nineteenth century, photography was vigorously asserting its ascendancy over [representative mediums like woodcuts, engravings, and lithography] in a way that echoes the tension between analog and digital technologies today" (Mahard 2003, 9). From its inception, photography has been closely related to science and technology. Baxter (2003) writes:

> As the technical side of photography evolved, the processes used had an effect on the intrinsic qualities of the images as well as the carrying medium: the machinery of photography affects the content of the photograph more than the machinery of typing affects the content of a letter.

Jammes and Janis (1983) write, "By situating the [photographic] discoveries within the evolution of science and technology, [inventors of photography] established a tradition that would mark every written account that followed: the story of photography would be the history of its technique" (xi). Panofsky (1937), in his famous essay discussing film, remarked: "It was not an artistic urge that gave rise to the discovery and gradual perfection of a new technique; it was technical invention that gave rise to the discovery and gradual perfection of a new art" (122). Technology is involved in every stage of photography: acquisition technologies capture the image, processing technologies transform the information into a reproducible product, distribution technologies provide access, and preservation technologies safeguard the content for long-term sustainability.

The prevalence and pervasive nature of digital imaging technologies requires an understanding of the changing information environment and the creation, management, use, and preservation of digital images. This chapter locates digital images in a continuum of photographic history and its key technical processes, and of the common formats that an information professional would encounter in visual collections.

Early attempts at photography

Prior to the invention of the camera, and as early as the beginnings of the Renaissance, artists have made extensive use of the *camera lucida* and *camera obscura* (literally 'light room' and 'dark room') to ensure accurate representation of landscapes and portraiture.

In the 1790s, Thomas Wedgwood (1771–1805), son of the English potter, devised a repeatable method of chemically staining an object's silhouette onto paper by coating the paper with silver nitrate and exposing the paper, with the object on top, to natural light, then preserving it in a darkened room. Similar to others' experiments to follow, these photographic images were not permanent. It is believed that as many as twenty-four people invented photography, from as early as 1782, working independently and using different methods, and moved by the "hitherto strange and unfamiliar desire to have images formed by light spontaneously fix themselves" (Batchen 1990, 9). In 1824, Antoine Hércules Romauld Florence (1804–1879), a Frenchman who lived in Brazil, discovered how to permanently fix *camera obscura* images with silver nitrate on paper. He referred to his process as *photographie* in 1834, at least four years before the English word 'photography' was coined. Three years after Florence, the Frenchman Joseph Nicéphore Niépce (1765–1833) took what he termed a heliograph, or sun drawing, an almost eight-hour long exposure of the courtyard of his house, from his attic window, using a light-sensitized pewter plate, creating a permanent direct positive picture which is now recognized as the first photograph.

French civil servant Hippolyte Bayard (1807–1887) invented his own photographic process, known as direct positive printing, and presented the world's first public exhibition of photographs in 1839. His process involved exposing silver chloride paper to light, which turned the paper black, then soaking the paper in potassium iodide before exposing it in a camera so that the light acted as a bleach. Bayard was persuaded to postpone his announcement of the process, which cost him recognition as one of the principal inventors of photography. In response to this injustice and the French government's failure to recognize his contribution, he took the first staged photograph, entitled *Self Portrait as a Drowned Man*, in which he pretended to have committed suicide (Lingwood 1986). Bayard's image represents the earliest photographic falsification, intentionally created to mislead observers.

Daguerreotypes and calotypes

"I have seized the light, I have arrested its flight," wrote Louis-Jacques-Mandé Daguerre (1787–1851) on the discovery in France in 1839 of the daguerreotype process (Gernsheim 1982, 22). These "mirrors with a memory," as Oliver Wendell Holmes called them, were direct positive images on a silver-coated copper plate. Daguerreotypes created highly detailed representations of the subject and, as such, appealed to the precision-oriented, positivistic attitudes of the time. Daguerreotypes, however, could not be reproduced as copies, used toxic chemicals, and were difficult to view from certain angles. Because they were vulnerable to physical damage from abrasion and to chemical damage from tarnishing, daguerreotypes were protected by a metal mat, covered in a glass rectangle of the same size, both of which were sealed with tape and fitted into a wooden, leather, or thermoplastic case lined with dark velvet. Daguerreotypes were often hand colored, and gold paint was added to jewelry. Not all cased photographs are daguerreotypes, which can be identified by their silvery, holographic appearance. The earliest daguerreotypes have laterally reversed images, since they are direct positives with no negatives. Although photographers could use mirrors or prisms to correct the images, exposure times often prevented this. Daguerreotypes required ten to fifteen minutes of exposure in bright sunlight, which was difficult for portraiture. Instead, static objects were often the subject for daguerreotypes, which suggests an underlying interest of photography to follow: the accurate recording of things, as part of a larger act of classification and possession.

The announcement of the discovery of the daguerreotype prompted the Englishman William Henry Fox Talbot (1800–1877) to publish his process for creating a negative from which an unlimited number of positive images could be produced. The calotype, from the Greek words for 'good' and 'impression,' was introduced in 1841 and was popular until the 1850s. The process involved brushing a silver-nitrate solution onto one side of a sheet of high-quality writing paper and then adding a potassium iodide solution. Once the paper negative had been exposed, it had to be developed for the latent image to be seen. The inexact chemical knowledge of the time affected the calotype's stability, causing it to fade, while the paper's grain produced a blurrier image than that of the daguerreotype. Calotypes required lengthier exposures, and the process itself took longer, since it required making first a negative, then a positive. However, calotypes could be reproduced, prints on paper were sturdier and easier to examine than daguerreotypes, and their tones were warmer. Talbot's discovery of the latent image, an invisible image produced by the exposure of the film to light, was epochal. Additionally, the calotype introduced photographic standards that are still used today: the negative–positive process and production of multiple positive prints.

Most photographers used daguerreotypes and calotypes for the next decade. By 1845, daguerreotype studios and traveling photographers were common. The daguerreotype remained the most common photographic process until it was replaced by the glass-plate negative and paper print in the mid to late 1850s. Its popularity both as an object and as a picture lay in its physicality, as it was small enough to rest in the palm of the hand. Its protective covers suggested how the image was prized and, because it was enclosed, mysterious. In comparison, a paper print, often affixed to a stiffened sheet of paper, appeared unsubstantial.

Despite its capacity to reproduce multiple copies, the calotype was not as readily accepted as the daguerreotype, especially for portraiture. Furthermore, by patenting his process, Talbot limited the calotype's commercial usage. Szarkowski (1983) notes the cultural differences between the daguerreotype and the calotype:

> The standard early technique for photographic portraiture in the United States was the daguerreotype, while in Europe it was the calotype. With the calotype system, an almost infinite number of prints could be made from a single negative, whereas the daguerreotype produced one unique picture. The distinction corresponded perfectly to the social perspectives of the United States on the one hand and, for example, England on the other. In England almost everyone wanted a picture of Lord Tennyson, Dr. Livingstone, or the queen, so such pictures were published in sizable editions. In the United States, by contrast, almost everybody wanted a picture of himself and his family. (238)

Technical developments

During the 1840s, developments that reduced exposure times and improved image definition for daguerreotypes and caloypes made portraits, landscapes, urban views, and panoramas possible. Armed with added precision and speed, photographers were eager to experiment with new techniques, "motivated by the desire to display and to glorify; to romanticize and to give pleasure; to inform, to record and to catalogue; and to preserve and to reform" (Lambert 1977, 66). Other impetuses include the desire to make easily reproducible images without the laborious practices of the handcrafted image. Art historian Wolfgang Kemp noted that photography is "the outgrowth of a broad spectrum of energies moving along in the same direction in philosophy, art, science, and economy; realism, positivism, and materialism are some of the terms for these epochal tendencies" (Koetzle 2008, 33). The naturalist and empiricist movements also influenced photography's development. Empiricism, the view that experience, especially of the senses, is the only source of knowledge and a fundamental part of the scientific method, developed at a time in the mid-nineteenth century when "photographic technologies and archival classification, embraced as tools of knowing, held the promise of control over an increasingly complex world" (Schwartz 2000, 5). Brown (1971) notes that photography's "entire history belongs within the industrial age, and that it seems to encompass both art and science, or at least to use science for artistic ends" (31). Benjamin (1936) suggests that the photograph is an example of "the work of art in the age of mechanical reproduction," an image based on both the chemical and industrial processes of production.

Photography liberated painting from the need to replicate reality because the medium was better equipped for exact representation and for capturing moods and moments. In doing so, it inherited such genres as the portrait and historical painting and contributed to the development of Modernism. Not only did photography dislocate time and space—an important feature of Modernism—but it also allowed access to the past through the visual information carried by the photograph and provided detail above that normally noted by the human eye.

McLaughlin (1989) adds that photography changed the world, compelling human documentation into a new world of information, and that its "ability to convey effectively complex information insures its legitimate historical comparison with movable type and telecommunications" (55).

One of the greatest inventions of the time that facilitated the communication of information was Samuel Morse's (1791–1872) electric telegraph, described as the 'Victorian Internet'; as it has formed "the basis of modern media and Internet services ... the network for the networked society began in the nineteenth century" (Standage 1998; Weller and Bawden 2005, 785). While securing his patents in England and France for this telegraphic device, Morse met Daguerre, whose work was attracting popular attention. Morse's description of the daguerreotype in 1839, the first account written by an American, was that it was "one of the most beautiful discoveries of the age." Morse, a portrait painter of considerable ability, was fascinated by the daguerreotype's adaptability to portraiture, despite the long exposure times. When he returned to America he set up his own photographic studio in New York, becoming the 'Father of American Photography.'

Other early formats

Introduced by the Englishman Sir John Frederick William Herschel (1792–1871) in 1842, cyanotypes were used until 1915. Printed on high-grade paper and lacking chemical complexity, cyanotypes are hardy and stable. Although they required long exposure times, the chemicals allowed cyanotypes to be prepared in subdued light, rather than in a darkroom. Cyanotypes were identified by their brilliant blue color, resulting from the mixture of chemicals in the salts used in this process, combined with exposure to light. The images could be produced by amateurs and the simplicity of the process made it very popular when it was first introduced. Its popularity picked up again in the 1880s because of the low cost of the images.

The collodion process, introduced by the Englishman Frederick Scott Archer (1813–1857) in 1851 and popular until the 1880s, resulted in a sharp image with commercial possibilities. The collodion process combined the high quality of detail of the daguerreotype and the reproducibility of the calotype with exposure times of as little as two seconds; it also made these previous processes obsolete.

The collodion process was the most complex of the early black-and-white photographic processes. The image was created using light-sensitive silver salts that were dissolved in collodion—a viscous solution of guncotton in ether and alcohol—and coated onto a glass plate. The plate was hand coated, and would be scraped clean and reused, and its negatives sometimes showed the photographer's thumbprint on the edge of the glass. The glass plate increased light sensitivity by twenty times, as compared to the earlier processes, resulting in a more brilliant and precise image. However, no fewer than eighteen steps were required, from sensitizing the plate to fixing the image. Additionally, since the plates had to be exposed while still wet, a photographer in the field had to travel with a darkroom. The result, however, was a well-defined negative capable of duplication, and the final print on albumen-coated paper was sturdier and cheaper than a daguerreotype and more permanent than a calotype. The invention of the process allowed cheaper alternatives to be developed, while the greater speed of image capture enabled photography to be used for the analysis of movement.

In 1877, Eadweard Muybridge (1830–1904) photographed horses in motion, using twelve cameras to record their gallop, trot, pace, and walk. The publication of the images caused a sensation because they showed that, during a gallop, all of the horse's feet are off the ground—which was different from what had been portrayed in paintings. Later, Muybridge projected the images onto a screen, creating the first motion picture. Szarkowski (1966) writes that Muybridge and the photographers who came after him "found an inexhaustible subject in the isolation of a single segment of time," discovering what Cartier-Bresson would later call "the decisive moment," an instant when the right elements are in place for a photograph to be taken before the scene returns to quotidian disarray (100).

In Boston, Massachusetts, James Ambrose Cutting (1814–1867) invented the ambrotype (from the Greek *ambrotos*, 'immortal,') by slightly underexposing a glass wet plate in the camera. The finished plate produced a negative image that appeared positive when backed with an opaque material such as velvet, paper, metal, or varnish. Ambrotypes were used primarily for portraiture and were faster and cheaper to produce than daguerreotypes. Ambrotypes were not laterally reversed, and because they were on glass they could be flipped over so that the emulsion was underneath. First produced in 1851 and popular until the mid 1860s, the ambrotype was sometimes called the 'glass daguerreotype' because the prints were housed in similar cases.

Tintypes, patented by Hamilton L. Smith (1819–1903) of Kenyon College, Ohio in 1856, were used until the 1910s. The photographic process was similar to the ambrotype, but the base was a thin sheet of iron with an opaque coating of black or chocolate-brown enamel. The lacquered sheet was coated with wet collodion emulsion containing silver salts just before exposure in the camera and had to be developed immediately. The finished image was usually laterally reversed. Their sturdiness, low cost, and fast exposure time, coupled with a growing

Figure 1.1   Ambrotype, front and back

(a) (b)

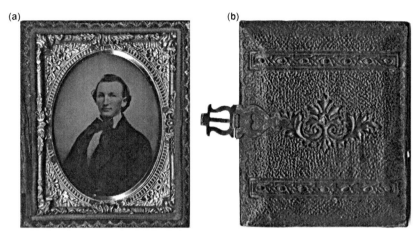

Note: The ambrotype is a glass negative that, when backed with a dark material, appears to be a positive. Its milky collodion highlights, which would appear black in a modern negative, are light and the unexposed areas show the dark backing. In this image the man's cheeks are hand-painted pink and his coat buttons are gold. Easier and cheaper to make than daguerreotypes, ambrotypes were presented in the same style of binding and case. Case components can help in dating the image, so long as they are original to the photograph. Over the glass is a sheet-brass mat, a metal support, and a gold-plated protector. To secure these elements, the completed ambrotype was placed in the right portion of a case lined with velvet-covered cardboard. In this example, the left portion of the case is missing. The back of the wooden case shows an embossed leather leaf design with a small lyre and heart-shaped clasp.

Source: Ambrotype, recto and verso, 3 × 2½ in (7.6 × 6.4 cm). Author's collection.

number of traveling photographers, caused tintypes to flourish. Szarkowski (1983) writes, "Photography reached voting age [with tintypes], and an advanced degree of technical competence, just in time to photograph the most tragic and traumatic episode in the history of the United States: the Civil War" (241). Soldiers posed for military camp photographers and mailed the images home.

Nicéphore Niépce's cousin, Abel Niépce de Saint-Victor (1805–1870), invented albumen negatives in 1847. Three years later, Louis Désiré Blanquart-Evrard (1802–1872) developed albumen prints made from salted egg white and sensitized with silver nitrate, which were used from 1850 to around 1890. The gold chloride toner and aging of the albumen often caused the photographs to have a yellowed, crackled surface. Most albumen prints were mounted because they curled easily. Albumen printing paper continued to be used until the turn of the century, when it was replaced by gelatin paper.

| Figure 1.2 | Tintype with damage |

Note: Unprotected tintypes typically suffer such damage of the kind exhibited in this hand-tinted studio portrait, with scratches, abrasions, and emulsion losses.

Source: Tintype, recto, 4 × 2½ in (10.2 × 6.4 cm). Author's collection.

Commercial expansion

From the beginning, photography was perceived as an ideal method of remembrance. Portraits were given to family, friends, and acquaintances; *memento mori* pictures were taken of the recently deceased; and people carried photographs of their loved ones with them. Oliver Wendell Holmes expressed the sentiment of the time when he wrote in 1861, "Those whom we love no longer leave us in dying, as they did of old. They remain with us just as they appeared in life; they look down upon us from our walls; they lie upon our tables; they rest upon our bosoms" (14).

The commercial expansion of photography provided greater flexibility in terms for size, pose, and presentation. By 1853, most cities and large towns hosted portrait studios—New York City alone had eighty-six (Newhall 1964). An article by Lady Elizabeth Eastlake in an 1857 issue of the *Quarterly Review* announced that "fifteen years ago ... specimens of a new and mysterious art were first exhibited to our wondering gaze," but now, "photography has become a household word and a household want" (Clarke 1997, 47).

One popular photographic development was the *carte-de-visite* or visiting card, a 4¼-inch by 2½-inch albumen-print portrait mounted on a thick paper card, which was patented in France by André-Adolphe-Eugène Disdéri (1819–1889) in 1854. The format allowed different poses to be printed on a single sheet, cut apart, and mounted individually. The *carte-de-visite* proved remarkably popular, especially in the 1860s, allowing naturalism and variety at a low cost, so that even the working classes could sit for their pictures and own the pictures of others.

Figure 1.3   *Carte-de-visite*, front and back

(a)

(b)

Note: *Cartes-de-visite* were inexpensively produced in their thousands. Ordinary people traded their collected images of family and friends, as well as pictures of famous people. In the original of this image, the woman's cheeks are painted pink. The wetstamp, indicating the name of the photographer and the location of his studio, can be useful in determining provenance. The two-cent stamp, found on the back of many cartes, is a United States tax stamp required from 1864 to 1866.

Source: Albumen print *carte-de-visite*, recto and verso detail, 4 × 2½ in (10.2 × 6.4 cm). Author's collection.

"The photographic portrait quickly became a popular alternative to the painted portrait (except among the wealthy) and eventually all but replaced it" (Melin 1986, 54). The status of photographic likeness was not lost on Napoleon III, who interrupted his march to war against Austria to pose in Disdéri's studio in 1859.

Newly invented photographic printing machines allowed *cartes* to be widely sold and distributed, creating 'card mania,' the trading of images among friends and visitors. Around the same time, the first commercial photograph album was introduced (Welling 1976). Personal photograph collections were common in the 1860s, as families displayed photographs of family members, landscapes, and famous people. By the early 1870s, *cartes-de-visite* were supplanted by cabinet cards, which were larger albumen prints (6¼ inches by 4½ inches) mounted on a cardboard backing and displayed in people's homes. Card photographs, whether *cartes-de-visite* or cabinet cards, were often decorated with information about the photographer and the address of the photographer's studio.

Development of image collections

Beyond personal collections, image collections were also developed to educate and entertain. Photography, coupled with the industrial-age improvements such as the high-speed printing press, rapid transport, and the development of photogravure (an intaglio print-making process) and halftone printing, allowed for the reproduction and distribution of images. Photojournalism developed as early as 1842, when wood engravings in news weeklies were modeled from photographs, and images of the Crimean War and the American Civil War appeared in popular magazines (Newhall 1964).

The rapid acceleration of image production allowed for the formation of image collections. Visual materials acted as surrogates for first-hand experience of places, people, and things, the perfect medium for depicting everyday life in both local places and distant lands. "In the nineteenth century, an age voracious for information, the camera immediately became its traveling eye" (MacDonald 1980, 34). People's knowledge of the world was increasingly derived from pictures, and memories of events became more closely associated with images of them. Photography became a carrier of facts, a democratic means of representation of daily life.

Disdéri predicted the "establishment of central photographic collections, international exchange, the massive diffusion of cheap art

Figure 1.4 Albumen print

Note: Painted scenery and accessories created an assortment of aesthetic backdrops for studio sitters, depending on the style of the time. In this image the hypnagogic background complements the angelic appearance and dress of the subject.

Source: Albumen print, recto, 5½ × 4 in (14 × 10.2 cm). Courtesy of Mary Lynn Ventola.

reproductions, all the conditions in fact for a museum without walls" (Fawcett 1986, 200). Photographs "made the whole world of art—painting, sculpture, architecture ... available to everyone, eliminating past restrictions of physical and social access," functioning as a "communicator to coordinate, control, and transmit all manner of information [aiding] in the teaching of skills and accumulation of knowledge" (Melin 1986, 54; McLaughlin 1989, 55). Institutions began to consolidate their power through the collection and dissemination of images; collections of stereographs, lantern slides—and later, in the twentieth century, 35mm slides—facilitated transmission of pedagogic knowledge.

Stereographs feature two photographs or printed images positioned side by side, about two and half inches apart, one for the left eye and one for the right. Viewed through a stereoscope, a device for viewing stereographs, the two flat images appear to combine into a single three-dimensional image, creating a remarkable illusion of depth. Used primarily from 1851 to the 1940s, the earliest stereographs were daguerreotypes, and the rarest were tintypes, although all photographic processes could be used for making stereographs. Glass transparencies and paper prints were the most suitable, as they could be handled easily and produced *en masse*. For example, in 1858 the London Stereoscopic Company offered 100,000 different views (Holland 2009, 129). Oliver Wendell Holmes, an enthusiastic collector of stereographs, predicted in 1859 that they would be:

> classified and arranged in vast libraries, as books are now ... We do now distinctly propose the creation of a comprehensive and systematic stereographic library, where all men can find the special forms they particularly desire to see as artists, or as scholars, or as mechanics, or in any other capacity. (60)

Produced to be viewed with a magic lantern, a forerunner of the modern slide projector, lantern slides were home entertainment and an accompaniment of traveling lecturers from the 1860s to the 1930s, when they were replaced by the more convenient 35mm slides. Lantern slides are positive transparent images on glass, usually albumen or collodion emulsions, protected by a second layer of glass which is secured with black paper tape. They would be fitted into a slotted wooden case with an accompanying script. Gustafson (2005) writes:

> Lantern slides are important historical artifacts not only in terms of date of manufacture, but also as original photography produced for teaching by providing factual evidence of what students were looking at in class at a given time period ... a lantern slide collection represents the physical manifestations of art historical inquiry, research, and pedagogy. (23–24)

Lantern slides played a significant role in the development of numerous academic disciplines, especially in the history of art, architecture, and the allied arts. Slide collections were first assembled at Princeton in 1882, Harvard in 1896, and Columbia in 1912. Beginning in 1905, horse-drawn wagons delivered lantern slides and visual collections to public schools as part of a US-wide visual instruction movement (Snow 2002). Large public visual collections were established after World War I.

Lantern slides were the primary materials in visual collections during the second half of the nineteenth century and the first half of the twentieth century, to be replaced by 35mm slides after their introduction in the 1930s. Early adopters preferred the ease of production, use, and transport of 35mm slides, as well as their full color, while others, questioning their stability and clarity, preferred the continued usage of highly detailed black-and-white or hand-colored lantern slides. "The issues that constituted the debate about maintaining dual collections … could constitute important evidence and clues for today's charged debates" over analog and digital images (Snow 2002, 6). Unfortunately, this transition period has not been researched fully. Even today, issues of dual collection formats continue, as Fry (2007) notes:

> Not until the images, the words, and the presentation method become as ubiquitous, as visually effective, and as dependable a system as the 35 mm slides, the well-organized and cataloged image collection, and the Kodak slide projector can we truly say that the digital transition … has been accomplished. (18)

The transition of the collection format from lantern slides to 35mm slides continued into the 1950s and 1960s. From this time on, 35mm slides predominated until around 2005, when digital technology gained popularity.

Plate and camera improvements

The ever-increasing need to educate and entertain with photographs provided impetus for yet other photographic discoveries. The disadvantage of collodion photography was the need to coat the glass plate, make the exposure, and develop the latent image to produce a negative before the collodion had dried. To ease their work, photographers searched for a dry, pre-coated plate with a sensitivity comparable to that of wet collodion.

In 1871, Richard Leach Maddox (1816–1902), an English photographer and physician, invented a method of preparing gelatin emulsion dry plates. Unlike the wet collodion process, dry plates needed less exposure to light and could be stored before use; they were used from the 1880s on. By 1895, gelatin silver prints had generally replaced albumen prints because they were more stable, did not turn yellow, and were easier to produce. Gelatin silver prints were the most usual means of making black-and-white prints from negatives and they remained popular for a variety of applications well into the twentieth century. Freed from the encumbrance of equipment and chemical knowledge, dry-plate photography made hand-held cameras and roll film possible. Brown (1971) writes:

> The continued development of the camera and processing of film as well as revolutionary advances in methods of mass reproduction at the turn of the century opened a new world of advertising and journalism—the rise of what we call mass media—for which photography was so naturally endowed. To this should be added the somewhat later evolution of the cheap, fool-proof camera which spawned a race of amateur photographers. (32)

By 1880, George Eastman's (1854–1932) Kodak camera made picture taking as easy as its slogan, "you press the button, we do the rest." The affordable camera was purchased with the film pre-loaded; after the pictures had been taken the customer returned the camera to Eastman Kodak, where the film was processed. Eastman Kodak then returned the processed photographs, together with the reloaded camera. Eastman invented not only a camera, but a system that produced standardized, mass-market photographs, domesticating and industrializing photography at the same time. Szarkowski (1966) writes that the medium:

> was easy, cheap and ubiquitous, and it recorded anything: shop windows and sod houses and family pets and steam engines and unimportant people. And once made objective and permanent, immortalized in a picture, these trivial things took on importance. By the end of the century, for the first time in history, even the poor man knew what his ancestors looked like. (7)

At the same time as the invention of the Kodak camera, the half-tone plate was introduced, shepherding in "the era of throwaway images," and allowing the "economical and limitless reproduction of photographs in books, magazines, and advertisements, and especially newspapers" (Tagg 1988, 56). In 1903, telegraphic transmission of half-tone images became possible, and in 1907 the *Daily Mirror* launched a photo-telegraphy service (Harvie, Martin, and Scharf 1970).

Along with the Kodak camera, the invention of the gelatin dry plate and film brought improved cameras to the amateur market. Kodak introduced the Brownie camera, costing a dollar or five shillings, in

Figure 1.5   Gelatin silver print

Note: Photographs can serve as excellent *tranche de vie* documentation of activities and issues. Despite its skewed composition, this snapshot of a proud mother and fretful child on a summer's day is endearing. As the main character in the movie *One Hour Photo* (2002) says, "If these pictures have anything important to say to future generations, it's this: I was here. I existed. I was young, I was happy, and someone cared enough about me in this world to take my picture."

Source: Gelatin silver print, recto, 2¾ × 4½ in (7 × 11.4 cm). Author's collection.

1900, making photography available to all, even children. The phrase "candid camera" was coined in the mid 1920s, when small, lightweight, precision cameras, such as the Ermanox, were introduced. Noiseless, smokeless flashbulbs were developed, allowing work in poorly lit conditions. The Leica camera, first introduced in 1925, transformed possibilities in photojournalism, achieving a state of portability and speed appropriate for capturing historic events.

Film developments

While nineteenth-century photographs did not make use of film as we came to know it during the late twentieth century, the discovery of synthetic plastic in 1869 laid the foundation for the development of transparent film (Bereijo 2004). Nitrocellulose was used to make the first photographic film, developed by Hannibal Goodwin (1822–1900), an Episcopal priest from Newark, New Jersey, in 1887, and introduced by Eastman Kodak in 1889. Later in the nineteenth century, the Lumière brothers, Auguste Marie Louis Nicolas (1862–1954) and Louis Jean (1864–1948), lived up to their names (*lumière* = 'light') and made cinematic projection possible using nitrocellulose film. However, the film is highly flammable, burning to produce carbon monoxide, and the fire cannot be extinguished with water because it is fed by the oxygen released by the burning nitrate. Tightly packed roll film, as used in motion pictures, is more combustible than individually wrapped sheet negatives. Despite its instability, the film remained popular until the 1950s.

Cellulose acetate film, introduced in 1930 by Eastman Kodak to replace nitrate film, is still produced today for movies, roll film, color negatives, and slides. Sometimes referred to as 'safety film,' cellulose acetate film can be identified by the word 'safety' embossed along its edge. In time, the film base shrinks, causing the emulsion to buckle and acetic acid to be released inside the plastic, causing a sharp odor of vinegar. Later, cellulose diacetate and cellulose triacetate were introduced (Bereijo 2004).

Polyester film, developed in 1965 and used to the present day, is inherently more stable chemically than either nitrate or acetate film. While nitrate and acetate film can be torn, polyester cannot, except with great effort. It is difficult to cut on traditional splicing equipment, so the acceptance of polyester base for cinema films has been slow. Today, most sheet film, excepting color, and most microfilm is on a polyester base.

Color photography

From the earliest days of photography, attempts were made to produce color. Many early photographs were hand colored using powders, watercolors, or thinned oil paints. Color photography depends on the principle that any color is represented to the human eye by a combination of the three primary colors—blue, green, and red—and that colors can be reproduced by adding together portions of the primary colors (known as RGB) or by subtraction using filters of the secondary colors cyan, yellow, and magenta (known as CYM).

The first true color photograph was produced by the Scottish physicist James Clerk Maxwell (1831–1879) in 1861, but it was not until 1907 that the Lumière brothers invented Autochrome, a commercial color process that became widely available. The process used glass plates with black-and-white emulsions that were coated with minute particles of starch dyed in primary colors and which, after processing, produced a colored positive transparency.

Other processes were developed and widely used, opening the field for cheaper, more readily available developments in color photography. In the early 1940s, commercially viable color films were brought to the market, most notably Kodachrome for 16mm film and 35mm slides in 1935, Kodacolor film in 1942, and 126 or 110 cartridge film for the popular Instamatic series of Kodak cameras in 1963 (Mora 1998). These films used the modern technology of dye-coupled colors in which a chemical process bonds the three dye layers (RGB or CYM) to create a color image. Further innovations included the development in 1972 of the first instant color prints from Polaroid (Ritzenthaler et al. 1984).

Until the 1970s, color photography was largely eschewed by professional photographers, who believed that the color lessened the photograph's veracity as a documentary image. Black-and-white images were equated with realism and authenticity, while color remained suspect. Today, the majority of photographs are in color. The preservation of color materials is more complicated than that of black-and-white media, due to the instability of chromogenic processes. Light, temperature, and relative humidity affect the permanence of the dyes used in color photography.

Digital technology

The beginnings of digital technology can be traced as far back as December 1947, when Bell Laboratories scientists John Bardeen, Walter Brattain, and William Shockley invented the transistor. The Nobel Prize-winning discovery started a revolution in the electronics industry and led to the replacement of vacuum tubes and mechanical relays with transistors that amplified and modulated electrical current. Transistors led to the development of integrated circuits, then microprocessors, which are the key component of digital imaging.

Developments continued in the 1950s. The SEAC (Standards Eastern Automatic Computer), the first computer that could store information electronically instead of on punched cards or on tape, was created in 1950. A year later, UNIVAC I, the world's first commercial computer, was put into service by the U.S. Census Bureau. At the same time, the Video Tape Recorder (VTR), which used electronic impulses to record images on magnetic tape, was developed at Bing Crosby Laboratories. In

1956, Shockley Semiconductor Laboratories began experimenting with silicon crystals, giving rise to a nascent computer industry. A year later, Russell A. Kirsch and his colleagues at the National Bureau of Standards constructed a mechanical drum scanner and used it to trace variations of intensity over the surface of photographs.

Digital imaging technology advanced significantly in the 1960s, with new advancements for defense in the Cold War. In response of the Soviet Union's launch of the first satellite, Sputnik, the U.S. National Aeronautics and Space Administration (NASA) program was established. The ability to transmit images across vast distances via radio waves was a requirement for space exploration. Beginning in 1959, the Corona Project launched spy satellites that used digital technology to beam photographs back to Earth. As early as 1964, NASA scientists used digital image-processing techniques to remove imperfections from images of the moon's surface, and were processing images of the moon from the Ranger 7 mission and of Mars from the Mariner 4 mission (Green 1989). Four years later, digital enhancement gave clarity to images of the Surveyor 7's footpad resting on the dust of the moon (Mitchell 2001). In the decades that followed, NASA improved the quality and resolution of its images, enabling it to produce brilliantly hued images of Jupiter, Venus, and Neptune.

Digital imaging continued to mature. In 1969, William S. Boyle and George E. Smith of Bell Laboratories developed a solid-state computer chip, the CCD (charge coupled device), which converted light into electrical signals. In 1972, Texas Instruments patented a filmless electronic camera. Three years later, Kurzweil introduced the first CCD flatbed scanner, and Eastman Kodak produced one of the first CCD still-image cameras, which recorded photographs onto a videotape cassette. In 1979, a scientific team from the University of Calgary, in conjunction with Fairchild Semiconductor, developed the Fairchild All-Sky Camera, the earliest digital camera used in the field.

The development of the personal computer, the falling costs of computer equipment, and the increasing storage and processing capacities of computers resulted in continued research into and development of computer graphics. As a century before, with advent of the Kodak camera, the 1980s saw the burgeoning technology of digital imaging give rise to a mass medium. Canon, Nikon, and Sony marketed compact still-video cameras that recorded images onto miniature floppy discs, first for professional use, then for the consumer market. In the late 1980s and early 1990s, digital cameras that recorded images in digital format directly onto disk or memory cards were developed. By the 2000s, cell phones that could fit in a person's pocket and that cost no more than $100 could take photographs of the same quality as digital cameras that cost $1,000 only a decade before. By 2003, cell phone cameras were outselling digital cameras. The technology of the digital camera was driven by both scientific and consumer requirements, leading to today's ubiquitous usage of digital technology.

By the mid 1980s, photographic-quality image-processing systems appeared, made possible by the growth of computer power, including Hell GmbH's Chromacom, Quantel Paintbox, and Scitex's Response System. In 1987, Thomas Knoll, a computer science PhD candidate, teamed with his brother John to create image processing software called Display, later renamed ImagePro. In 1990, it was released as Adobe Photoshop. Photoshop and other similar software applications made increasingly powerful photograph-manipulation tools available to anyone.

Anticipating the future of digital photography at this time in its history would be similar to predicting developments in analog photography in the 1860s. Historically speaking, changes have occurred in response to innovations in photographic materials and processes. In previous transitions, competing technologies were available for a time, but ultimately the new technology overtook its predecessor. While it is not clear how quickly the current evolution will resolve, it seems likely that traditional photography will increasingly represent a smaller segment of the photographic industry. Indeed, digital images have such overwhelming advantages that they will most certainly succeed analog photography as the primary visual medium, much in the same way that photographs surpassed handcrafted images in the nineteenth century. Information professionals must keep abreast of changes in the photographic industry in order to maintain collections that can move into the future, while being responsive to the long-term needs of collections and their users.

2

Digital image basics

Abstract: Archivists, curators, and libraries working with contemporary image collections need to understand the basic technologies and processes involved in building a cohesive set of digital images, together with the information required to access, preserve, and manage them. This chapter imparts the fundamentals of digital images, comparing the distinct characteristics of digital and analog images and the usefulness of digital surrogates of analog originals. Definitions of and recommendations for dynamic range, bit depth, resolution, master and derivative files, interpolation, compression, and file formats are given, with the needs of information professionals in mind. The purpose of the chapter is to present necessary information on the use of digital imaging to convert and make accessible visual cultural heritage materials.

Keywords: bit depth, digital images, dynamic range, image file formats, master and derivative files, resolution

A very fine photographer asked me, "What did it feel like the first time you manipulated an image?," and I said "Do you mean the first time I shot black and white instead of color, do you mean the first time I burned the corner of a print down, do you mean the first time I 'spotted' a dust speck on my print, do you mean the first time I shot with a wide angle instead of a normal lens, I mean what are you referring to? Where does it stop?" (Dan Burkholder, 1997)

Today, as we enter the post-photographic era, we must face once again the ineradicable fragility of our ontological distinctions between the imaginary and the real, and the tragic elusiveness of the Cartesian dream. (William J. Mitchell, 2001)

Man Ray's Rayographs and Moholy-Nagy's photograms had succeeded in removing the camera from the center of the visual experience. Might we not then ask, particularly here in the digital domain which is the Internet, whether we are now entering a new era of an even more direct aesthetic experience. An era of "photography-less" photography, where film, print and camera alike are replaced by pixels cemented in an electronic matrix. Where the distinction between photography and painting—once hotly debated—has evaporated, as both are reduced to infinitely replaceable pixels hurdling through cyberspace. (John Noon, 2003)

Introduction

As early as 1972, John Berger wrote in *Ways of Seeing*, the seminal art history text, that images had "become ephemeral, ubiquitous, insubstantial, available, valueless, free. They surround us in the same way as a language surrounds us. They have entered the mainstream of life over which they no longer, in themselves, have power" (32). Elkins (1999) continues, "What makes twentieth-century culture so different from that of past centuries is not only the quantity of images … but the kind of images we create and consume" (84). Both authors commented on the pervasive nature of analog photography, but the volume and omnipresence of digital images has even more far-reaching corollaries for our visual culture.

"It is the artist who is truthful and it is photography which lies, for in reality time does not stop," remarked Rodin. The decisive moment captured in digital media may be lengthened and amplified by connecting it to other images online. In this way, digital photography, even more so than its analog predecessor, embodies nonlinearity and asynchronicity and serves as an initial recording, susceptible to modifications and recontextualization. As Willis (1990) writes, "Digitization is a process which is cannibalising and regurgitating photographic … imagery, allowing the production of simulations of simulations" (199). Digital photography represents an essentially different approach than analog photography, as the fidelity of the mechanical age is replaced by the fluidity of the digital.

This chapter provides an overview for information professionals of the fundamentals of digital images and summarizes key differences between chemically based and digitally produced images that will influence the creation and management of image collections of the future.

What is a digital image?

A digital image is an electronically processed picture composed of data, a "representation of an image stored in numerical form, for potential display, manipulation, or dissemination via computer technologies" (Terras 2008, 6). Digital files rely on a sequence of discrete numeric values, the most common being binary, typically 0 or 1. An electronic pulse is denoted by a 1, while 0 represents its absence. A bit (short for binary digit) is a single binary value, the smallest unit of data in a computer. Eight bits form a byte, the unit most computers use to represent a letter, number, or typographic symbol. Strings of bits can represent text or images.

Digital images are created in two ways. They can be born digital, originating in digital form in cameras, cell phones, or digital imaging software. As early as 2001, Wiggins estimated that an astonishing 93 percent of material was born digital (14). Alternatively, digital images can result from digitization, in which photographic negatives, prints, or transparencies are scanned into a computer.

In the context of this book, a digital image is understood as a bitmap or raster image, the common, two-dimensional format generated by a digital camera or scanner, composed of pixels, which combine to make a continuous-tone image. Bitmap images result from the conversion of analog data into digital data by a measuring process known as sampling. This digitization process analyzes the value of the analog data at intervals and converts the tessellation of information into bits that the computer can interpret. The greater the amount of sampling, the greater the quality of the resulting image.

The word 'raster' originates from the Latin *rastrum* or 'rake,' from the pattern of parallel lines resembling those that the tool makes on the earth. The parallel lines of the scanned raster image form the image projected on the cathode-ray tube of a television set or display screen. When images started to be stored in computers, the term 'bitmap' replaced 'raster' because the images are 'mapped' by the information stored in bits.

Vector graphics, geometrical objects such as those created by drawing software or computer-aided design (CAD) systems, are not explored in this book. Bitmapped images are far more prevalent than vector images in archives, libraries, and museums, and in personal collections, and therefore require the serious attention of information professionals.

Digital and analog differences

Digital technology has become thoroughly assimilated into photography, uniting photography and computer-generated imaging; photographic archives and online databases; and the camera, the internet, and mobile media. Despite the pervasiveness of digital images, there are significant dissimilarities between analog and digital images that affect their management in heritage institutions both now and in the future.

Figure 2.1 Hybrid imaging flowchart

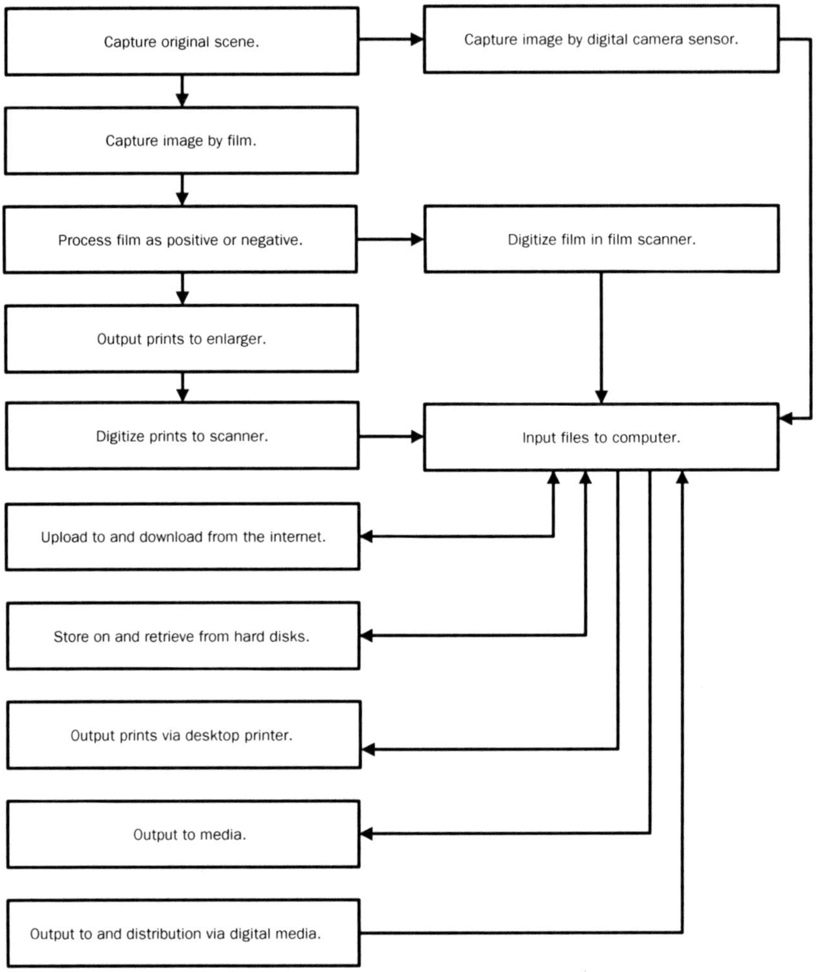

Capture original scene.	→	Capture image by digital camera sensor.
Capture image by film.		
Process film as positive or negative.	→	Digitize film in film scanner.
Output prints to enlarger.		
Digitize prints to scanner.	→	Input files to computer.
Upload to and download from the internet.	←	
Store on and retrieve from hard disks.	←	
Output prints via desktop printer.	←	
Output to media.	←	
Output to and distribution via digital media.	→	

Note: This flowchart illustrates how analog and digital images are captured or converted in today's hybrid environment.

A major difference from the analog process is that photographers are able to select and edit digital images in their cameras. Whereas analog roll film contained a record of all images taken in a single photo shoot, with digital photography this is no longer the case. How this editing will influence image collections in future is unclear but, as Howe (2001) observed, "In the era of digital photography, for example, the picture of President Clinton hugging an insignificant intern [Monica Lewinsky] would never have been found. It simply would not have been preserved" (26).

The effortlessness, sophistication, and undetectability of photographic image manipulation is unprecedented in photographic history. "Once lauded by nineteenth-century commentators for its ability to reproduce reality without the intervention of man's flawed hand, photography now offers even the most bumbling of amateurs the opportunity to alter the image" (Miller 2007, 12). Images can be "seamlessly altered, blended and mixed together," making "anything possible," because "the essential characteristic of digital information is that it *can* be manipulated easily and very rapidly by computer" (Sanders et al. 2000, 2; Mitchell 2001, 7). De Perthuis (2005) writes, "In the digitally manipulated image there is no original. Instead, the solid elements of the conventional photograph are dissolved into a kaleidoscope of pixels that, like the chorus line from a Busby Berkeley musical, are easily choreographed into endless permutations" (409).

Photographic production has shifted from the chemical darkroom to computer software, and the manipulation of the image, not its capture, has become more important. Images can be altered by adding or subtracting elements, increasing or decreasing focus, modifying lighting, or extending the image's borders. Unlike conventional retouching, electronic changes are immediate and undetectable. Within this elastic sense of space and time, the decisive moment is no longer when the photographer took the picture, but when the image is modified.

The photographer is thus reduced to the position of supplier of raw materials that will be refined by the picture editor who controls what is seen (Bate 2001). In 1989, photography's sesquicentennial year, it was estimated that 10 percent of color photographs published in the United States were digitally retouched or altered (Ansberry 1989). Undoubtedly, this percentage has increased, as commercial photography is now overwhelmingly digital.

Analog images are transcribed from one set of physical properties into another, analogous set. Digital images, however, are converted, as their physical properties are represented by a binary code. Analog images are inseparable from the surface that carries them; they are medium specific, bound by their materials and techniques. Digital images are created using one binary code for all media, enabling convergence and conversion. Marsh (2009) comments, "With the advent of digital data ... we have surpassed the photograph and entered into the realm of the matrix along with its mathematical connotations" (268).

Digital files do not exist as material objects, and "the lack of physical connection between a digital photograph's subject and image suggests digital images function as pure iconicity" (Dzenko 2009, 19). Doane

(2008) states that digital images, as a "medium without materiality, of pure abstraction incarnated as a series of zeros and ones, sheer presence and absence," have emerged as "the apparent endpoint of an accelerating dematerialization, so much so that it is difficult not to see the very term digital media as an oxymoron" (9).

From a digital project perspective, the most important difference between chemically based and digitally produced images is that analog images have continuous tones, whereas digital images are divided into discrete, measurable, and exactly reproducible elements. Unlike in analog photographs, which vary spatially and tonally at a constant rate, the fine details and smooth curves in digital images are approximated on the pixilated grid, and continuous tonal gradients are broken into steps. "The basic technical distinction between analog (continuous) and digital (discrete) representation is crucial here," notes Mitchell (2001). "Rolling down a ramp is continuous motion, but walking down stairs is a sequence of discrete steps—so you can count the number of steps, but not the number of levels on the ramp" (4). In traditional photographs, enlargement reveals more detail, but a grainier picture. Digital images cannot be enlarged beyond a certain point because they have limited spatial and tonal resolution; they reveal their microstructure as their pixels become more prominent.

Digital images as surrogates

Digital images can act as surrogates of the original, analog item. Digital surrogates are superior to past surrogate forms, such as microfilm, because they can be delivered via networks, enabling enhanced access to simultaneous multiple users in dispersed locations. Digitized images can be effectively indexed for accurate identification and instantaneous retrieval, thereby eliminating time-consuming manual searches through slide drawers and print files. Physical proximity to digital image collections is unnecessary, unlike for analog collections.

Digital collections online "provide enriched intellectual control of images, multiple points of access, and enhanced image manipulation" (Matusiak 2006, 479). Thumbnails can be mounted on websites as reference copies of the originals, and images from different institutions can be displayed together. Increasingly sophisticated linked webs of information combine images, metadata, captions, and annotations. As Burns (2006) comments, "scalability, functionality, usability, sustainability, and preservation are the issues of the day in an environment clearly in a state of rapid change and expansion" (131).

Online collections of digital surrogates increase access in a variety of ways, especially for images in high demand and with key historical or intellectual content. Additionally, the availability of collections online may increase demand for, or interest in, items that have been relatively unknown. New viewing experiences are possible by browsing through a collection, allowing for a completely different type of intellectual access to visual information. Digital collections can reinstate into circulation material that had been withdrawn for conservation or security reasons. Digital surrogates can add functionality to the way a collection has traditionally been used, such as enabling analysis of damaged material. Digital surrogates can halt the loss of information over time. Huyda (1977) states, "The instability of the photographic medium runs counter to the archival objective of permanence and requires increased technological support. The expanding use of photographs [in research] raises tendentious issues of archival protection versus researcher access" (5). The availability of digital surrogates satisfies most users' research needs. However, access via the internet brings wider knowledge of the existence of items, which, ironically, can lead to more research requests to view the originals. Digitization is "a self-promoting vehicle: the more that is provided, the more the resource is used, and the higher the demand for other resources of high quality" (Terras 2008, 123). If preservation is an issue, high-resolution surrogates and sufficient hardware and software in the institution's reading room will allow for satisfactory access. Additionally, as visual collections become more vulnerable to damage, or as their monetary value and susceptibility to theft increase, the current trend toward greater restrictions on access to the originals will accelerate. Preservation and access can be achieved with digital surrogates, making it possible to retire the original material under access restrictions, extending its life for future generations. To put it simply, "Some objects *must* be viewed in surrogate form only" (Smith 2003, 13).

Digital surrogates allow for deeper study than do their analog originals, enabling scholars to view details that the photographer may have never seen. Digitization restores "to photography its documentary, evidentiary quality, even as it translates emulsion to binary code, changing the materiality of the image but restoring its referent with greater detail than ever before" (Volpe 2009, 14). However, with digitized images, researchers risk losing information that allows them to understand how the image was used and how its physicality changed over time.

The availability of an inexhaustible supply of identical copies, what Barthes (1981) calls photography's ability to "reproduce to infinity [what] has occurred only once," is an important consequence of digitization (77). Surrogates can be generated for specific purposes in formats such as JPEG for web display, TIFF for storage, and PDF for print reproduction. The millionth copy of a digital image is indistinguishable from its progenitors. "A digital copy is not a debased descendent but is absolutely indistinguishable from the original" (Mitchell 2001, 6). Electronic copies suffer no degradation through the duplication process, unlike other copy formats, such as facsimiles of analog photographs. A copy of a digital photograph is indistinguishable from its source, such that the term 'original' loses its meaning in this electronic world.

Digital cameras and scanners

Whether born digital or digitized, electronic images are created by either a digital camera or a scanner. Depending on the image collection and the resources available, institutions should use the best equipment that they can afford, with the highest resolution and greatest dynamic range. In many cases, digitization is outsourced to a vendor, making the purchase of digital equipment unnecessary, though an understanding of the technology involved is still needed.

Digital cameras differ from traditional cameras in that a light-sensitive silicon chip called an image sensor, usually a CCD or CMOS (complementary metal oxide semiconductor) sensor, replaces film. Although CCD sensors are expensive and run on a relatively high voltage, they deliver a clean signal with low noise. CMOS sensors, typically used in webcams and phone cameras, require a great deal of processing to produce a clean, noise-free image. As a result, relatively few digital cameras use CMOS chips, but those that do are renowned for the high quality of their images.

Image capture is based on a grid of red, green, and blue color filters arranged in a Bayer pattern—named after its inventor, Bryce E. Bayer of Eastman Kodak. The filter pattern is 50 percent green, 25 percent red, and 25 percent blue, because the human eye is most sensitive to green light.

Photosensitive diodes on the surface of the image sensor convert light passing through the lens into electrical impulses, which are measured and converted into a digital number; the more light, the greater the impulse.

The final image is composed of a mosaic-like grid of picture elements known as pixels, which are similar to dots on a newspaper photograph. Each pixel is created when a color and brightness measurement is taken from a given position in the image and recorded as a discrete number. This binary number holds instructions for recreating the pixel with a specific brightness and color. The information is stored as digital data in a memory device that is either built into the camera or in the form of a removable card. The data is translated by software programs for display on the camera's LCD screen or on a computer monitor.

Most scanners work by moving a scanning head across the picture to recreate the image inside the computer. Flatbed scanners have a large glass plate on which the photograph is placed, face down, to be scanned. A linear CCD on a moveable bar, with a single row of diodes (or three rows for red, green, and blue) scans the image area. Quick and economical, flatbed scanners allow for bitonal, grayscale, and color scanning and often come with their own scanning software.

Film scanners are essentially flatbed scanners with a light source that transmits light through the film to the sensors. Many flatbed scanners claim also to be slide scanners, which is true to a degree, as one can use a template to fix the slide in position on the glass and then scan the area of the image. However, the resolution may be poor, exacerbated by the fact that the slide is raised, albeit fractionally, above the surface of the glass.

With color negatives, scanners must be able to separate tonalities that are extremely compressed in the shadows. Density is normally very low, with the result that light transmission is high; the scanner sensors work with relatively bright light. In addition, color negative materials have an orange mask that must be neutralized in order to obtain lifelike colors.

In contrast, color transparences have high densities, so the scanner must be able to discriminate subtleties with low transmission and low light. Scanners need a large dynamic range and high bit depths to be able to scan both types of material. As a result, film scanners produce better scans than do flatbed scanners that have been converted to scan film.

Drum scanners provide the highest quality, resolution, and dynamic range, but are expensive, require great skill to operate them, and are rarely found outside dedicated scanning agencies. With these scanners, the analog image is secured with tape onto the circumference of a rotating glass drum. A photomultiplier converts the reading taken from the narrow beam of light into a digital signal, at one pixel width for each revolution. In addition to varying the sampling rate or resolution of the drum scanner, the scanning technician can also set the aperture, which enables the film grain to be rendered sharp or soft, as required.

Dynamic range and bit depth

The human eye can distinguish millions of colors, all of which arise from two types of light mixtures: additive or subtractive. The former involves adding together different parts of the light spectrum, while the latter involves the subtraction or absorption of parts of the spectrum, allowing the transmission or reflection of the remaining portions. Computer monitors use an additive system, while print color creation is subtractive. This fundamental difference can complicate the accurate reproduction of images on a computer monitor or the printing of digital images.

Dynamic range is the span of tonal difference between the lightest light and darkest dark of an image. The higher the dynamic range, the more potential shades can be represented, although the dynamic range does not automatically correlate to the number of tones reproduced. Dynamic range also describes a digital system's ability to reproduce tonal information. For photographs, this capacity may be the single most important aspect of image quality.

Color depth is also known as sample depth or bit depth, because digital color values are internally represented by a binary value. The number of bits used to represent each pixel, or the number of bits used to record the value of each sample, determines how many colors can appear in a digital image. Higher color depth gives a broader range of distinct colors. However, the more color information that is captured and stored, the higher the resulting file size.

A bitonal image is represented by pixels consisting of one bit each, which can represent two tones, typically black and white. The inability to represent intermediate shades of gray limits the bitonal image's usefulness; black and white analog images should be captured in grayscale to ensure that the tonal range of the original is represented.

Images in 8-bit grayscale are constructed from 256 tones, with 0 being black and 255 pure white. With so many intermediate levels of gray

Table 2.1 Bit depth and tones

Number of bits	Number of tones
1 (2^1)	2
8 (2^8)	256
16 (2^{16})	65,536
24 (2^{24})	16,777,216

present, the human eye is unable to detect any changes. An 8-bit grayscale is recommended for capturing and representing printed text, music manuscripts, hand- or typewritten papers, photographs, and graphic arts where color is not an important attribute (Library of Congress 2007). Capturing color information when it does not contribute any additional information to the surrogate only increases file size and is unnecessary.

For color image capture and storage, 4-bit color representing 16 colors per pixel, 8-bit color representing 256, and 16-bit color representing 65,536 are not advocated because of their limited color range. Instead, a 24-bit color image can be created from a palette of 16 million colors, capturing a spectrum beyond the range of human perception. A 24-bit color display is currently the highest bit depth available on affordable monitors. As a result, 24-bit color is recommended for archival-quality color images.

Although 32-bit color and 48-bit color are possible, such images tend to be converted to 24-bit color after capture. A 32-bit display actually consists of 24 bits of color data and 8 bits of 'alpha' or transparency data. For archival purposes, 48-bit color can be used so as to preserve as much of the original data and detail as possible. The use of 48-bit color extends color capacity to 280 trillion colors. The extra bits capture differences in light and shade more accurately. However, the file sizes that are generated when dealing with these bit depths are prohibitively large and are well beyond the recommendations for color information capture.

Resolution

Digital image resolution refers to the quantity of visible detail described in pixel dimensions, such as 640 by 480 pixels, the horizontal dimension preceding the vertical. Dots per inch (dpi), measuring the number of individual dots of ink a printer can produce per linear inch, or pixels per inch (ppi), measuring the number of pixels per linear inch, are common terms to express resolution. If a digital image is three inches wide, and the total number of pixels across is 900, the resolution of the picture is 300 pixels per inch, expressed as 300 ppi or 300 dpi.

Often, there is confusion between dpi and ppi because cameras create images based on pixels, while printers depict pixels using ink dots. To add to the confusion, camera and printer manufacturers tout resolution as a key factor of image quality. For example, a printer with a resolution of

1200 by 4800 dpi may seem to have a high resolution, but the first value is the maximum number of dots that it can apply in one horizontal inch. The second, vertical value refers to how small an increment the printer motor pulls the paper through before placing the next line of ink dots.

Similarly, a scanner's resolution may be 3000 by 1500 ppi. The horizontal resolution is fixed by the number of sensors available, while the vertical resolution is determined by the increment that the sensors can shift, in this case 1/1500 inch or 1500 ppi.

Screen resolution refers to the number of pixels shown on the entire screen of a computer monitor, which depends on a combination of monitor size and display resolution setting. Monitor size usually refers to the diagonal measurement of the screen, although its actual usable area is typically less. For example, an 800 by 600 pixel screen will display 800 pixels on each of 600 lines, or 480,000 pixels in total. An image displayed at full size on a high-resolution screen will look smaller than the same image displayed at full size on a lower-resolution screen.

Rather than the number of pixels per inch, camera resolution is usually the maximum resolution that a digital sensor can achieve. For example, a grid of 3072 by 2048 pixels in a sensor gives a total of 6.29 million pixels or 6.3 megapixels. Megapixels are the standard unit used by manufacturers when referring to camera resolution. More megapixels translate to more individual light sensors on the image sensor, higher image definition, and sharper pictures.

Resolution recommendations

Digital imaging hardware is capable of capturing all the information in photographic originals. Such a high quality standard produces digital images that are versatile in terms of their potential uses, but requires the storage and manipulation of large files. A lower quality standard produces files that are more manageable but often limits their utility for publication or exhibition. Selecting the appropriate quality level depends on analyzing the desired uses of the images over the long term. For instance, low-resolution images may be sufficient for classroom use by undergraduates, but would be inappropriate for conservators assessing details.

Although images are often viewed on monitors, projectors, or other low-resolution devices, they should be captured and digitized at the highest quality that is practical. It is easy to transform a high-resolution image into a lower-resolution one by reducing the image size and

Figure 2.2 Digital imaging recommendations

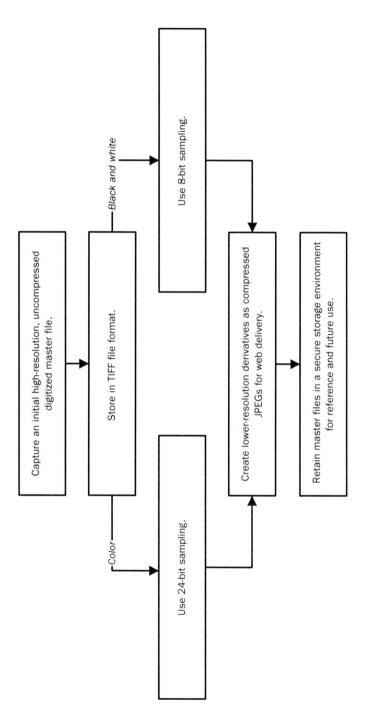

Capture an initial high-resolution, uncompressed digitized master file.

Store in TIFF file format.

Black and white

Use 8-bit sampling.

Color

Use 24-bit sampling.

Create lower-resolution derivatives as compressed JPEGs for web delivery.

Retain master files in a secure storage environment for reference and future use.

Table 2.2   Master-file resolution and bit depth guidelines

Original object	Minimum recommended resolution	Bit depth
Black and white text documents	600 pixels/300 ppi	8-bit gray
Microfilm, black and white	600 pixels/300 ppi	8-bit gray
Oversized materials	600 pixels/300 ppi	24-bit color or 8-bit gray
Illustrations, photographs, maps, manuscripts	600 pixels/300 ppi	24-bit color
35mm slides or negatives, black and white	6000 pixels on longer side/3000 ppi	8-bit gray
35mm slides or negatives, color	6000 pixels on longer side/3000 ppi	24-bit color
Large-format photographs, transparencies, or negatives	6000 pixels on longer side/3000 ppi	24-bit color

discarding pixel information, but it is impossible to do the reverse without causing pixilation.

However, digitizing at the highest possible quality is not always feasible. Kenney and Chapman (1996a) advise:

> The "full information capture" approach to digital conversion is designed to ensure high quality and functionality while minimizing costs. The objective is not to scan at the highest resolution and bit depth possible, but to match the conversion process to the informational content of the original—no more, no less. At some point, for instance, continuing to increase resolution will not result in any appreciable gain in image quality, only a larger file size.

Full information capture creates a digital replacement of the original in terms of spatial and tonal information content, which is defined by the film format, emulsion type, shooting conditions, and processing techniques. Ultimately, information content has to be defined, whether

Figure 2.3 Cabinet card

Note: Information professionals need to decide if the digital image should match the analog image's current state or if its original appearance should be reconstructed—in the example of this image by removing the discoloration and chipped edges. It should also be determined if additional information should be captured, such as the blind stamp on the front that reads "Lelly Studio 329. Lexington St., Baltimore, MD," or the handwriting on the back that identifies the sitter as "Mr. Theodore Olmstead, Jeweler on Lexington St."

Source: Albumen print cabinet card, recto, 8½ × 4¼ in (21.6 × 10.8 cm). Author's collection.

based on human perception, on the physical properties of the original, or on a combination of both.

Additionally, image quality can be compromised in order to enhance system performance. The full quality of the image stored is often not reflected in display, as most display devices are capable of far less resolution than printers are. The higher the quality of the image, the more storage it will occupy and the more system resources it will require, including higher bandwidth networks, more memory in workstations, and longer and costlier scanning. File size in bytes can be determined by the following equation:

> Horizontal ppi × vertical ppi × bit depth × original item's width in inches × original item's height in inches/8.

Digitizing everything within a collection at high resolution and in full color would be uneconomical. However, if the resolution is too low, the surrogates will be a poor likeness of the image they represent.

Monitors display images between 72 and 100 ppi, depending on the type and quality of the display, with top models displaying 200 ppi, in which the pixels appear to the human eye to blend, presenting a smooth image. If preparing images primarily for screen display, such as on a website, low resolution is suitable. Placing low-resolution images online has the added benefit of preventing use of the images for commercial printing.

Printed images require 300 dpi to replicate the sharpness of conventional photographs. Most inkjet printers are capable of producing 300 to 1200 dots per inch. When producing digital images for printing, it is useful to know the printing technique and output resolution.

Master and derivative files

Digital image files are commonly divided into master and derivative versions. Master files are the highest quality available, usually the originals created by the sampling process. The scans are rich enough to use for several different purposes and are created to obviate the need to rescan the original. From these images, lower-quality copies create more easily distributed access files. Master files should be digitized at 600 to

300 ppi and saved as uncompressed TIFF images. Thumbnail and other smaller-scale images, such as those suitable for online delivery, can be produced from these master files as 72 ppi JPEGs. Rare or fragile material should be scanned just once, creating a high-resolution image from which other, smaller images can be derived, thus ensuring that the original material is subjected to as little handling and light exposure as possible.

Interpolation

If a digital image is resized without increasing or decreasing the number of pixels, the resolution of the image changes. For example, a 900 by 900 pixel image that is three inches wide has a resolution of 300 ppi. Each square inch contains 300 by 300 or 90,000 pixels. If the image is resized to six inches wide, without increasing the number of pixels, the 900 by 900 pixel image now has a resolution of 150 ppi, as the 900 pixels are stretched over six inches instead of three inches. Each square inch contains 150 by 150 or 22,500 pixels. Conversely, if the size of the image is decreased without changing the number of pixels within the image, the resolution of the image increases.

Interpolation is the process of creating missing data, often used to create new pixels to insert into an image or to choose which pixels to delete from a resized image so as to maintain image resolution and ensure that the image does not become pixilated. Interpolation is also referred to as resampling, upsampling (if increasing the number of pixels), or downsampling (if decreasing the number of pixels).

New pixels can be calculated through pixel replication, where one pixel at the lower resolution is made into multiple pixels in the higher-resolution image, or through pixel generation, using the average of the color values of the two pixels on either side of the one required. More sophisticated algorithms calculate the values of new pixels by assigning values based on those are already in the image. When an image is increased in size by interpolation, new information is inserted that was not part of the original image. Likewise, if the image is decreased in size, original information is discarded. This raises questions of authenticity, particularly if the image is to be used for research purposes. The labor-intensive image capturing process will not have to be repeated in the future if the images are created at a high resolution at the outset.

Compression

Compression algorithms reduce the number of bytes required to represent data and the amount of memory required to store images. Compression allows a larger number of images to be stored on a given medium and increases the amount of data that can be sent over the internet. It relies on two main strategies: redundancy reduction and irrelevancy reduction.

Redundancy reduction, used during lossless encoding, searches for patterns that can be expressed more efficiently. An image viewed after lossless compression will appear identical to the way it was before being compressed. Lossless compression techniques can reduce the size of images by up to half. The resulting compressed file may still be large and unsuitable for network dissemination. However, lossless compression does provide for more efficient storage when it is imperative that all the information stored in an image should be preserved for future use.

Irrelevancy reduction, a lossy compression, utilizes a means for averaging or discarding the least significant information, based on an understanding of visual perception, to create smaller file sizes. Lossy compression reduces the image's quality but can achieve dramatic storage savings. It should not be used when image quality and integrity are important, such as in archival copies of digital images.

Not all images respond to lossy compression in the same manner. As an image is compressed, particular kinds of visual characteristics, such as subtle tonal variations, may produce what are known as artifacts (unintended visual effects), though these may go largely unnoticed, due to the continuously variable nature of photographic images. Other kinds of images, such as pages of text or line illustrations, will show the artifacts of lossy compression more clearly. These may accumulate over generations, especially if different compression schemes are used, so artifacts that were imperceptible in one generation may become ruinous over many. This is why uncompressed archival master files should be maintained from which compressed derivative files can be generated for access and other purposes.

File formats

File formats ensure that data is stored according to a predictable set of rules that will allow for device independence, so that files can be shared or accessed on other systems. Information professionals must consider the long-term usefulness and accessibility of the images and choose a file format that is a non-propriety industry standard. Doing so will ensure the enduring viability of the digital images, which is important because, due to the costs of digitization, it is unlikely that the process will be repeated in the short term. Additionally, standard formats ensure the maximum re-usability of images across projects and over time, and enable institutions to take part of cooperative projects and to make the best use of staff expertise. Adopting open international standards also enables the institution to make best use of external sources such as advisory boards, contractors, and consultants.

Despite the range of file formats, only a few are recommended for image collections. The most common formats include TIFF (Tagged Image File Format), JPEG or JFIF (Joint Photographic Experts Group File Interchange Format), PNG (Portable Network Graphics), and GIF (Graphic Interchange Format). Many digital imaging projects use TIFF master files and JPEG derivative files.

The 'tagged' in TIFF refers to the internal structure of the format, which allows for arbitrary additions, such as custom metadata fields, without affecting general compatibility with photo editing and management programs. These tags describe the size of the image or define how the image data is arranged and identify the compression algorithm that is used. TIFF supports several types of image data compression, allowing an organization to select the most appropriate for its needs. Many users of TIFF opt for a lossless compression scheme such as Lempel-Ziv-Welch (LZW) encoding, to avoid degradation of image quality during compression. Users often avoid any compression at all, so as to ensure that image data will be simple to decode. TIFF is the best file format for archiving high-quality images because files can be edited and saved without damage to the image due to compression loss.

JPEG is a lossy compression format that allows image data to be compressed by assigning a compromise color value to a block of pixels rather than to each separate pixel. The extent of this process can be controlled, but there is irretrievable deterioration in image quality, most noticeably in smooth-gradient areas. JFIF specifies how to produce a file suitable for computer storage and transmission over the internet from a JPEG stream. JFIF does not allow for the storage of associated metadata, which has led to the development of SPIFF (Still Picture Interchange File Format), which can be read by JPEG-compliant readers while providing storage for more robust metadata. JPEG is best used with continuous tone photographic images, destined for email and web use, or for storage when space is limited. It is not suitable for use with line drawings or text because its compression method does not perform well with these types of image.

PNG (pronounced 'ping') is an open source standard that was introduced to overcome the possible patent problems associated with the GIF format. It is used either as an 8-bit indexed version, a 24-bit color version, or an infrequently used 48-bit version. A versatile format, it offers the advantages of lossless compression in full color and a GIF replacement in 8-bit form. However, it cannot compete with JPEG in terms of producing high-quality images for web viewing. The compression available from PNG in 24-bit mode creates a file of about 60 to 75 percent of the original size.

GIF is an 8-bit (and under) indexed file type with a range of 256 colors. It works best with simple images using block colors, such as graphics, logos, and banners. GIF uses lossless LZW compression, but the amount of compression will depend on the type of image being saved. A full color, continuous tone image is unlikely to compress to less than 30 percent of its original size. The GIF file format also supports layers, allowing for both transparency and animation.

Some cameras use unprocessed RAW formats. These files include the original data captured by the sensor without alteration, and adjustments can be made on the computer to the white balance, exposure, and sharpness before saving them in a non-proprietary format. Raw processing combines maximum flexibility with image brightness and white balance and removes the limitations of fixed, in-camera processing, such as sharpening. RAW files usually contain higher bit depths than the equivalent JPEGs and TIFFs produced by the camera. The RAW format is often called a 'digital negative' because little camera processing has been applied to the image. Since no standards exist, the RAW files must be opened in that format with an image editor capable of translating them.

Digital decisive moment

Marion (2006) notes that with digitization:

> photography has reopened its eyes, relearning a new distinct place for itself that is undefined because prior roles have been appendaged. This is the post-reality in which photography seems to be; it is neither a place of stasis nor of flux. As experimental as its historical traditions, photography remains true to its amorphous, experimental self. (36)

We have entered the digital decisive moment, where digitally produced images have substantially departed from the legacy of chemically based photographs, in ways in which information professionals are still trying to understand. Fontcuberta (2003) notes, "The dramatic metamorphosis from the grain of silver to the pixel represents nothing more than a screen which conceals the evolution taking place in the whole framework that provided photography with a cultural, instrumental and historical context" (10–11).

Traditionally, changes in photographic equipment have always led to alterations in production. The first portraits required subjects to remain motionless for minutes at a time, until emulsion sensitivity improved to allow for shorter exposures that tolerated movement. When cameras became portable and efficient, they allowed for the decisive moment when photography stops time, the "simultaneous recognition, in a fraction of a second, of the significance of an event as well as the precise organization of forms which gives that event its proper expression" (Persinger 2007, 10).

This moment has now expanded, connecting to other moments online, providing a visual construction of ideas, contributing to human understanding, and supporting a global range of cultural and artistic interests. With this in mind, managing a collection of analog, digitized, and born-digital images requires decision making in order to apply limited resources toward maximum usability and accessibility for years to come. Each institution must form a strategy to serve its unique needs. However, an understanding of the rudiments of digital images, as well as the fundamental distinctions between analog and digital images, may make management easier for information professionals charged with preserving visual heritage.

3

Photographic image issues

Abstract: Using a postmodern perspective, this chapter discusses the many levels of meaning that images hold simultaneously, urging that photographs must be managed with their context intact. The chapter explores some of the challenges facing information professionals as they endeavor to understand and make accessible the contextual meanings of analog, digitized, and born-digital photographic records. Through its refined notions of what constitutes authenticity, postmodernism offers information professionals an orientation by which to consider the photographic process, to better appraise, preserve, and represent images. Understanding context and connotation improves the ability to provide deeper description of visual holdings and make them more useful and usable to scholars. Additionally, other issues that affect the management of image collections, such as intellectual property rights, legal and cultural considerations, ethics, and preservation, are explored.

Keywords: authenticity, contextual meaning, copyright, postmodernism, preservation, visual literacy

Photography never lies: or rather, it can lie as to the meaning of the thing, being by nature tendentious, never as to its existence. (Roland Barthes, 1981)

A photograph is a universe of dots. The grain, the halide, the little silver things clumped in the emulsion. Once you get inside a dot, you gain access to hidden information, you slide inside the smallest event. This is what technology does. It peels back the shadows and redeems the dazed and rambling past. It makes reality come true. (Don DeLillo, 1997)

A photograph is usually looked at—seldom looked into. (Ansel Adams)

Introduction

Images play an important role in our cultural history and form an integral part of the collective memory preserved by archives, libraries, and museums. Reflecting broader, societal attitudes, information professionals have been limited in their interpretation of photographs as historical evidence beyond the image's subject content. Only since the 1970s have they begun to treat photographs as the complex documents that they are.

The traditional reliance of scholars on the written and spoken word has given way to photographs' being regarded as valid historical evidence. The information that images provide to their viewers and their capacity to evoke the past have earned them growing recognition as source materials for the study of history. Now, influenced both by an increased visual literacy and by a postmodern emphasis on the limitless circumstances of human actions, greater understanding of photographs examines the context in which they have been created, used, and maintained in image collections. Additionally, the rise of the historical study of social movements and under-represented segments of society in the mid-to-late twentieth century increased the usage of visual materials in scholarly work (Kaplan and Mifflin 2000). Furthermore, the development of digital media and the deeper exploration of the concept of provenance have increasing relevance for further developments in image collection methodology.

This chapter explores some of the challenges facing information professionals as they endeavor to understand and make accessible the contextual meanings of analog, digitized, and born-digital photographic records. Understanding context and connotation enhances the ability to provide deeper description of visual holdings and to make them more useful and usable to scholars. In addition, the chapter explores other issues that affect the management of image collections, such as intellectual property rights, legal and cultural considerations, ethics, and preservation.

Visual literacy

Information professionals must develop their own sense of visual literacy. Visual literacy is "an evolving concept best defined as the ability to think and learn in terms of images" and is a reaction to the awareness that "contemporary culture is increasingly captured by and reflected in visual ... documents" (Kaplan and Mifflin 2000, 73). The proliferation of images means that increasing numbers of visual records will enter archives, libraries, and special collections—but information professionals and researchers often lack skills to evaluate and understand them. Pacey (1983) notes, "There is of course a crucial difference between illiteracy and visual illiteracy. People who cannot read know that they cannot read. We all think we can 'read' images—but very probably we cannot," but information professionals need to be "highly visually literate themselves, and to be aware of the implications of visual illiteracy in others" (233). When historians are trained:

> The criticism of visual evidence remains undeveloped, although the testimony of images, like that of text, raises problems of context, function, rhetoric, recollection whether soon or long after the event, secondhand witnessing and so on. (Burke 2001, 15 as cited in O'Toole and Cox, 2006, 200 n. 54)

Library science and archival programs also lack visual education components, and their students:

> seldom ask the most basic questions about [a photograph's] physical form, internal articulation, purpose of intellectual result … [consequently] subject content is erroneously conflated with their message, issues of representation are ignored, and informational value is equated only with visual fact. (Schwartz 1995, 44)

Additionally, the text-based training of information professionals has often caused them to "'read' pictures 'literally' without being aware of certain rules and conventions that are in sharp contrast to the rules of alphabet, grammar and syntax" (Taylor 1979, 420).

Within the wider scope of society, advertising utilizes nonverbal language through a proliferation of manipulated images. In the aesthetics of advertising, images transition from representations of products to branding designed to manipulate consumers' experiences and perceptions so as to motivate them to purchase goods. A lack of visual literacy in the public leaves the concepts and values inscribed in such imagery unchallenged. Visual literacy is not encouraged in society, because if one knew how to read images, the subliminal messages of advertising would be more evident and less compelling.

Despite the wide spread of visual illiteracy, Schwartz (1995) stresses that information professionals must:

> rethink the nature, production, and purpose of photographs as documents in order to achieve a contextual understanding of their

use by governments, businesses, and individuals to convey government policy, communicate corporate ideology, construct national identity, shape collective memory, establish symbolic space, and define concepts of self and the cultural Other. (42)

In order to consider photographs as records of enduring value, it is important to change the way images are managed within cultural heritage institutions. It is essential not to view photographs as decontextualized items, valued only for their aesthetic qualities. Instead, their meaning is discovered by uncovering their context. Visual literacy through a postmodernist lens affords a flexible perspective, as it welcomes a wide range of contextual information as a basis for understanding and managing photographs in image collections so as to make their multiple meanings accessible to users.

Levels of meaning

Images bear "their meaning not in natural language, but in the arrangement of their colors, shapes, textures, dimensions—in short, their physical and visual attributes" (Woll 2005, 20). Viewing a photograph involves a series of ambiguous, polysemic meanings, which relate as much to contextual clues and the viewer's experiences as to the photograph itself. Photography is highly interpretive, ambiguous, culturally specific, and heavily dependent upon any contextualization provided by text and layout. Images are "simultaneously generic and specific," "almost infinitely divisible and can carry an almost inexhaustible range of meanings," and lack "a 'hierarchy of authenticity' to which all matters of interpretation may be referred" (Shatford 1986, 47; Sutherland 1982, 44; Homberger 1988, 734). Burgin (1982) writes:

> The intelligibility of the photograph is no simple thing; photographs are *texts* inscribed in terms of what we may call "photographic discourse," but this discourse, like any other, is the site of a complex intertextuality, an overlapping series of previous texts "taken for granted" at a particular cultural and historical conjuncture. (144)

Finnegan (2006) argues that image description is inherently subjective, requiring complex conceptual and ideological processes to determine the subject. Image collections "function as terministic screens, simultaneously

Figure 3.1 Gelatin silver print of family group

Note: Photographs have multiple levels of meanings: denotative and connotative; ofness and aboutness; pre-iconographic, iconographic, and iconologic; and superficial, concrete, and abstract. While most viewers would find limited meaning and description in this 1950s family portrait, its meaning to me is significantly different, as it depicts my father (center), my uncle, and my grandparents.

Source: Gelatin silver print, recto, 2½ × 3¼ in (6.4 × 8.3 cm). Author's collection.

revealing and concealing 'facts,' at once enabling and constraining interpretation" (118). Interpretation is needed because, as Huyda (1977) writes, "existing captions are often incomplete, inaccurate, deliberately distorted or irrelevant. For photographs with no captions, the task of identification is even more difficult. Recognition by memory or through comparison with other visual evidence is often inadequate and unreliable" and "the attribution of photographs to particular photographers or studios is a complicated process" (10).

Barthes (1977) suggests an important distinction between the relative meaning of elements within the photographic frame, distinguishing between the denotative and the connotative. Denotative is the literal meaning and significance of any element in the image. The connotative aspects of the image display a series of visual languages or codes, which are themselves the reflection of a wider, underlying process of signification within the culture.

Another way to describe Barthes' perspective on visual engagement would be the 'ofness' and 'aboutness' of an image. 'Ofness' is what an image objectively represents, its superficial perception, whereas 'aboutness' is what it subjectively represents. This second level of representation requires "more complex ways of thinking about the images and requires specific historical knowledge of circumstances or events, participants, techniques, and more" (Kaplan and Mifflin 2000, 79–80). Most collections are structured around the experience of looking *at* something, rather than looking *for* something, which entails greater cognitive effort. For example, museums often use 'ofness' groupings to organize their collections into categories of art movement, style, or artist rather than ascribed viewer 'aboutness' meanings such as landscapes, heroic acts, or the color blue.

Panofsky (1939) identifies three levels of meaning: pre-iconography, iconography, and iconology. Pre-iconologocial description identifies the primary or natural subject matter, the objects and events represented in the image. For example, a painting depicts a seated woman with a landscape behind her. Iconographical analysis involves secondary or conventional meaning and requires a cultural familiarity that goes beyond everyday knowledge of objects and events. For instance, iconography recognizes the woman in the painting as Lisa di Antonio Maria Gherardini del Giocondo of sixteenth-century Florence. Iconological interpretation identifies the intrinsic meaning of content, requires a synthesis of pre-iconographical and iconographical information derived from the image itself, as well as knowledge about the artistic, social, and cultural setting to which it belongs. For example, the composition and background of the painting Leonardo da Vinci's *Mona Lisa* echo previous paintings of a seated Madonna, which were widespread at the time of its creation.

Kaplan and Mifflin (2000) also describe three levels of meaning: superficial, concrete, and abstract. Like Panofsky's iconology, the abstract level draws upon analytical abilities and intellectual elements that are not easily expressed in words, requiring "a particular set of sensibilities and skills, and a knowledge base that, like facility with history and historiography, must be learned" (80). It requires expertise of the conventions and technology of visual perception, expression, and of the particular medium. Clearly, to interpret the meaning of images, it is necessary to be familiar with cultural codes in a postmodern milieu.

Postmodernism defined

Postmodernism "eschews metanarrative, those sweeping interpretations that totalize human experience in some monolithic way ... anything that reflects the past or present 'hegemony' of dead white males" (Cook

2001, 15). The postmodern stance "is one of doubtfulness, of trusting nothing at face value, of always looking behind the surface, of upsetting conventional wisdom" (Cook 1994, 317). Influenced by Marxism, feminism, psychoanalysis, semiotics, and other theoretical models, it is opposed to a formalist agenda, seeing it as both intellectually fruitless and politically conservative. As a philosophy, postmodernism rejects concepts of rationality, objectivity, and universal truth. Instead, it emphasizes the diversity of human experience and multiplicity of perspectives. In many ways, a postmodernist perspective is well suited to the utilization of photographic records, because it questions traditional notions of truth and the concept that records can have only one possible meaning.

Academic disciplines have contended with the challenges of postmodernism since the 1970s. Information professionals as well have questioned their own traditional stances of neutrality. The increase in archives and special collection repositories, graduate education programs, the impact of technology, and the greater emphasis on nontextual materials have given impetus to a re-evaluation of traditional principles and practices.

Some postmodern ideas have gained ground within the information professions, specifically with regard to archival selection and appraisal, as archivists recognize the subjectivity of deciding which records to preserve and which to destroy. However, postmodernism has made significantly less headway in the area of arrangement and description of records—particularly analog and digital images—where many orthodoxies still reign. Questioning the objectivity of these practices as well as understanding the influential role of information professionals is a step towards shaping a representative pictorial record of history.

Authenticity

The multifarious meanings of images have fueled postmodern discussions of the authenticity of the "extended, loaded evidence" of photography (Barthes 1981, 115).

From its invention, photography was thought to offer an "immediate, faithful and permanent record" documenting "the mundane, the trivial, the everyday texture of life so often ignored by more traditional records" (Brown 1971, 32; Leary 1985). "From the very beginning, it was the task of photography to testify to the (nearly) incredible. The mechanical, quasi automatic, aspects of the photographic process lent photographs their power as evidence" (Koetzle 2008, 60). For instance, Florence referred to his images as "drawings made by nature," Niépce called them "the copying of views from nature," and Talbot titled his first book *The Pencil of Nature*. Daguerre (1980) claimed that the daguerreotype was "not merely an instrument which serves to draw Nature; on the contrary it is a chemical and physical process which gives her the power to reproduce herself" (12). Later, photojournalist Lewis Hine said, "A good photograph is not a mere reproduction of an object or a group of objects—it is an interpretation of Nature, a reproduction of impressions made upon the photographer which he desires to repeat to others" (Koetzle 2008, 145).

Photography emerged when advances in technology and the sciences prompted confidence in the ability to master the world intellectually and physically. Thus, there was a belief in the power of photography to reproduce reality. "The goal of exact reproducibility through technology held a particular fascination" (Schwartz 2000, 23). Photographs were created by machines, which lent them credibility, whereas conventional reproductions, like engravings, were created by hand. Photographs were regarded as exact reflections of reality, and so a "faith was put in the photograph that has never been and could not be put in the older hand-made pictures" (Ivins 1953, 107).

Photographs are often perceived as neutral, objective records, devoid of subjective intention. "The visceral appeal of looking at people from the recent or remote past was powerful, and photographic records seemed more immediate—more 'true' somehow—than secondary descriptions" (O'Toole and Cox 2006, 30). Humphreys (1993) notes that:

> photography has been a focal point for concerns about the nature of subjectivity, authenticity, and representation itself ... photographic accuracy, with its emphasis on the copy and the reproduction ... promised to make concepts of the genuine obsolete and to devalue, both economically and symbolically, the original. (686)

Schwartz (2000) notes that photographs were believed to be "unmediated and, therefore unassailably truthful" (36). "Bearing witness is what photographs do best; the fact that what is represented on paper undeniably existed, if only for a moment, is the ultimate source of a medium's extraordinary powers of persuasion" (Goldberg 1991, 19). Berger and Mohr (1982) state, "It is because photography has no language of its own, because it quotes rather than translates, that it is said that the camera cannot lie. It cannot lie because it prints directly" (96).

However, photographs, for the most part, are no longer regarded as "truth-telling artifacts," nor as "a literal rendering of reality (a reproduction) but ... [as] an interpretation—a construction" (Mifflin 2007, 34; Ballard and Teakle 1991, 44). Neither were photographs a "facsimile of a total reality at some moment in time ... only a partial reflection" (Huyda 1977, 11). Vogt-O'Connor (2006) writes:

> Photographs are expressive and subjective documents whose content is selected to omit most of the visual world, framed in a camera viewfinder, focused to the photographer's interest, captured by a certain shutter speed, and recorded upon media that have speed limitations and certain color and tonality biases. Photographers may manipulate their images in the darkroom by airbrushing, cropping, dodging and burning, enlarging, hand-coloring, and retouching them to make the reality reflected in the image better fit the photographer's or client's wishes. (97)

To state it another way, "the convergence of photographer, subject, camera, and other variables, such as who is or isn't present, and the authority or influence they have" provides a restricted view of reality that must be examined (Mifflin 2007, 34). To view photographs as objective records ignores the cultural and social background against which the image was taken, just as it renders the photographer a neutral recorder of the scene.

Nineteenth-century photographs required a great deal of physical work, and perhaps for that reason photographers were less reluctant to manipulate the contents of their images. Even in the nascent days of photography, images were sometimes altered, often for artistic reasons. The emulsions of the time lacked the tonal range to capture both sky and foreground, so two exposures would be taken of a scene, and a single print created from the negatives. Similarly, photographers often altered their photographs to look like paintings by smearing grease on the camera lens or using special printing processes.

While photographs have always been contrived, they have also, simultaneously, been believed to be more real than other kinds of images. "Since the mid-1800s, the general population has considered photography a better representation of the external world than painting, despite logical

Figure 3.2 Cased ambrotype, front and back

(a)

(b)

Note: The authenticity of this ambrotype is questionable, making dating and determination of its context problematic. Images are usually placed in the right section of the miniature case, and the embossed velvet pads are normally glued to the left section. In this example, they are reversed. The different decorative styles on the outside of the case and the black linen repair tape that connects them indicate that this artifact may have been assembled from separate ambrotypes. The only determination of dating is from the mat style, used from the mid 1850s to early 1860s.

Source: Ambrotype, recto and verso, 3 × 5 in when opened (7.6 × 12.8 cm). Author's collection.

evidence to the contrary—until digital technology prompted a re-examination" (Shapter 2007, 2). As one critic has put it, "Digital technology does not subvert 'normal' photography because 'normal' photography never existed" (Manovich 2003, 245). Stiegler (2008) adds:

> Even digital photography, which planted the seed of ontological doubt into the heart of the image, has not radically changed our everyday interaction with images. We no longer believe in the objectivity of photography, but we do still regard photographs as, in some way or other, our reality. (197)

Ritchen (1999) laments, "Certainly subjects have been told to smile, photographs have been staged, and other such manipulations have occurred, but now the viewer must question the photograph at the basic physical level of fact" (11).

The connection between a photograph and its subject is 'indexical'—a term coined by philosopher Charles Sanders Peirce to designate the relationship between a signal carrying a sign and the sign's object. A photograph is a sign carried by the light reflected off the objects it represents. The easily manipulated digital photograph cannot be trusted to represent accurately a scene and, therefore, cannot be indexical. A manipulated image may be understood as illusory, but the experience of expecting a photograph to reveal reality produces dissonance for the viewer.

Asserting that the camera never lies is as erroneous as averring that the computer always does. That the digital medium allows for a seamless reconstruction and manipulation of reality seems to have heightened an awareness of the questionable nature of the authenticity of all images. Every photograph is altered in some manner by the intention of the creator, the technology involved, and the interpretation of the photograph by the viewer.

A key element of postmodernism is an understanding that photography has resigned its role as a privileged conveyor of information in favor of a position that concedes that reality is an evolving construction. The decline of photography's authority is tied to the abundance of images in everyday life, which has led to a depreciation of the medium's intrinsic believability. Crimp (1977) states:

> To an ever greater extent, our experience is governed by pictures, pictures in newspapers and magazines, on television and in the cinema. Next to these pictures, firsthand experience begins to

retreat, to seem more and more trivial. While it once seemed that pictures had the function of interpreting reality, it now seems that they have usurped it. (3)

Marien (2006) writes:

> Both digital ardor and digital angst owe to earlier Postmodern attitudes, which questioned the truth-value of traditional photography while simultaneously hailing the social power of mass media. By the nature of its production techniques, digital imaging seems to have undermined the authority of the traditional photograph as an index of the material world. (401)

No longer are images regarded as "mirrors with a memory," reflecting the workings of the world to viewers. The idea that reality has been replaced by its simulacrum, advanced by French philosopher Jean Baudrillard, is illustrated—literally—by the plethora of photographic images in Western culture. Batchen (1999) explains that there is a:

> pervasive suspicion that we are entering a time when it will no longer be possible to tell any original from its simulations. Thing and sign, nature and culture, human and machine—all of these hitherto dependable entities appear to be collapsing in on each other. Soon, it seems, the whole world will consist of an undifferentiated artificial nature, a hyperreal. According to this scenario, the vexed question of distinguishing truth from falsehood will then become nothing more than a quaint anachronism—as will photography itself. (207)

Baudrillard and Batchen believe that human experience has become so reliant on simulacra that it has lost contact with the real world on which the simulacra are based.

Decontexualization

The validity of photographic records has been further eroded by their different treatment from traditional textual records, which destroyed evidence of their provenance and original order—the maintenance of both of which are a fundamental archival principles (Boles 2005). Provenance is information regarding the origin, custody, and ownership of an item or collection; records of the same origin should be kept together to preserve their context. Original order is the organization of records as established by their creator. Maintaining records in original order preserves existing relationships and evidential significance that can be inferred from the records' context.

Despite photography's appeal, the medium was not always recognized as a primary source material, because in "the formative years of archives only written records were regarded as archival and deserving of preservation" (Ritzenthaler et al. 1984, 5). Photographs are often segregated from their originating records at acquisition, with arrangement and description being performed independently. Due to their chemical components, they may be stored in different environmental conditions. In large repositories, photographs are often managed by different staff and made available in a separate reading room. Without accurate records of the names, dates, and events depicted, images hold little historical value. The separation of photographs from their original order and provenance renders their usefulness as documentary evidence secondary to their aesthetic appeal. Schmidle (1996) notes, "Stripped of its original context, an old photograph is reduced to mere curiosity" (14).

However, unarchival practice is not alone in attritting meaning. Crimp (1995) argues that the entry of photographs into the privileged space of the museum stripped them of their evidential and informational significance. Part of the acceptance of photography in museums is purely economic: they are cheap to ship and display and often less expensive than other forms of media to purchase; they also attract visitors because they are more easily understood than other art forms.

Crimp (1995) criticizes the Museum of Modern Art, the New York Public Library, and the Victoria and Albert Museum for consolidating their holdings of photographs by separating them from their original holding departments and transforming them into aesthetic objects. He writes that the segregation of photographs "will no longer serve the purposes of information, documentation, evidence, illustration, reportage. The formerly plural field of photography will henceforth be reduced to the single, all-encompassing *aesthetic*" (75). Volpe (2009) adds, "Photographs still operate in the museum under assumptions of authenticity and transparency—photographs document authentic cultural rituals and authenticate the museum's objects unmediated by the cultures that produced them or that are their subjects" (11).

Photographs, if only considered as art objects, lose their plurality of meanings.

Sekula (2003) criticizes image collections in archives, libraries, and museums because they assemble and homogenize photographs, establishing a "territory of images" of "abstract visual equivalence" among heterogeneous images (444, 445). He writes:

> In an archive, the possibility of meaning is "liberated" from the actual contingencies of use. But this liberation is also a loss, an *abstraction* from the complexity and richness of use, a loss of context.... And so archives are contradictory in character. Within their confines meaning is liberated from use, and yet at a more general level an empiricist model of truth prevails. Pictures are atomized, isolated in one way and homogenized in another. (445, 446)

He continues, "Although the very notion of photographic reproduction would seem to suggest that very little is lost in translation, it is clear that photographic meaning depends largely on context" (445).

Paradigm shift

When photographs lose their context, they are reduced to their subject content. A content-oriented approach to photographs requires information professionals to have a certain level of expertise in various academic subjects in order to provide useful service to researchers. This was possible until the 1970s, when historical research began to change, moving towards greater interest in race, gender, political issues, labor, and the lives of everyday people. It was becoming increasingly difficult for information professionals to provide effective access to resources when that access was determined by the extent of their knowledge of an ever-broadening range of subjects. At the same time, the work of Roland Barthes, John Berger, Victor Burgin, and Susan Sontag re-evaluated traditional perceptions of photographs and influenced the expanding conception of contextual information by those charged with managing image collections. What was needed was an approach that would alleviate the need of information professionals to master the subject content of the records. Instead, a method that applied provenancial information would allow the broader interests of researchers to be served. The focus would need to shift from revealing record content to uncovering contexts.

Contextual meaning

"Never neutral, the photograph always finds itself attached to a discourse (or, more accurately, a cacophony of competing discourses) that gives any individual photograph its meanings and social values" (Batchen 1999, 9). Photographs are surrounded by historical, aesthetic, and cultural frames of reference and by a set of relationships and meanings related to the conventions of a particular place and time, the interests of the photographer and the original patron or client, and the intended function of the image. "Even a quick reading reveals interpretive tensions: the photographer's intentions clash with the ambitions of the subjects, and both appear at odds with the needs of the viewers, who bring to the image their own experiences and interpretive concerns" (Sandweiss 2007, 193). Gustafson (2005) asserts, "One cannot forget that every photograph, like every painting, is composed by its maker and designed to convey specific information. The objecthood of the [image] is not limited only to composition, but also extends to the context of production" (25). Berger and Mohr (1982) continue, "A photograph is a meeting place where the interests of the photographer, the photographed, the viewer and those who are using the photograph are often contradictory. These contradictions both hide and increase the natural ambiguity of the photographic image" (7).

In order to understand an image, "it is essential to know exactly where it was created, in the framework of what process, to what end, for whom ... and how it came into our hands" (Duchein 1983, 67). Information professionals "must be mindful of photographic intent, not because it provides the *only* way of interpreting an image, but because it provides one possible starting point for a more complicated reading of a picture" (Sandweiss 2007, 194). Adequately documenting the provenance of photographs requires more than simply identifying the creators, but also their social and cultural contexts, functions, and custodial history—in other words, their provenance.

"Like many principles ... [provenance] is easier to state than to define and easier to define than to put into practice" (Duchein 1983, 64). Nesmith (2006) writes:

> Provenance is still mainly viewed at its surface level—of fairly obvious formal and official information, such as the title of the creator(s), mandated functions, and organizational structures and links. There has been little exploration of their societal dimensions

and their place in archival theory and practice [but] acknowledging this more complex view of provenance brings archival theory and practice into line with broader intellectual life (352, 359).

The concept of provenance requires that photographic documents be understood "in context, or in relation to their origins and to other documents, not as self-contained, independent items, to be re-organized in archives along new subject, chronological or geographical lines" (Nesmith 1993, 2).

Determining context for photographs may be difficult because the subjects and photographers are often unknown, and the photographs themselves, originally part of a series, have become detached from their original function to end up in archives, libraries, and museums. Berger and Mohr (1982) explain:

Box 3.1   **Best practices for determining contextual meaning**

- Study the photographs, negatives, and their housings for written evidence.
- Check accompanying documentation for contextual clues about creators, subjects, place names, and time periods.
- Consult reference sources, both printed and online.
- Consider the images' physical characteristics, style, and genre.
- Look for similar photographs in the collection, which may provide more information.
- Discover clues in the photograph that could help to identify a place or time period.
- Think about the events or activities that might have led to the creation of the photograph, so as to discover the image's original purpose or function.
- Contact staff members at other repositories that specialize in the same subject area or type of photography.
- Ask the public for help in identifying creators or subject matter.
- Confirm information through multiple sources, so as to minimize the risk of recording incorrect information.

All photographed events are ambiguous, except to those whose personal relation to the event is such that their own lives supply the missing continuity. Usually, in public the ambiguity of photographs is hidden by the use of words which explain, less or more truthfully, the pictured events. (128)

A photograph's physical form, format, process, and size convey meaning. "The physical form of the photographic image, prescribed by prevailing technology, determines what can be photographed, how it can be displayed or published, how it can be encountered by others, how it can circulate through public culture" (Sandweiss 2007, 197). For instance, analog images are physical objects and, especially in the case of early, small photographic forms like daguerreotypes, often served as personal items rather than as objects for public display. In another example, Miller (2007) differentiates between the photographic albums of yesteryear and today: "Thick and clunky, wrapped in rough leather, [the albums] inspire awe due less to their grace than their bulk. The Victorians seem to have had a taste for *gravitas*, whereas twenty-first century citizens yearn for technologies that make life faster, sleeker, and more immediate" (9). Sassoon (1998) notes that the photograph's physicality:

has been an integral feature for a photographic object since the earliest photographic processes from which there was only a single tangible item produced. Embedded within the photographic object are clues visible to the trained eye which reveal the subtle relationships between negatives, printing papers, and processes used to physically produce the image. (6)

To put it differently, meaning is "not produced by the universalizing equalizer of the archive but by tracing the material conditions under which a photograph was produced, collected, and archived" (Volpe 2009, 11). Volpe (2009) writes, "The wide-scale digitization projects in museums and libraries are most definitely democratizing access to the nineteenth-century photograph: the web is the new archive and the desktop is the reading room. But is what we are seeing still a photograph?" (16).

Bearman (1995) suggests that the context for photographs should be examined through their relationships with information categories. These categories include the object "in itself," in time (its creator, collection, ownership, and collecting history), in place (its association with people, events, and locations), within the realm of ideas (its subject, association with other categories, and its embodiment of abstract ideas), and as part of a whole. He asserts that, "Because documentation is frequently not explicit about relationships that are evident from the context in which they are mentioned ... it may be necessary to analyze source materials to expose these relationships" (298).

Schwartz (1995) stresses that the study of a photograph must take into account the "terms of its relationships with the persons concurring in its formation" who created "mediated representation of reality; the product of a series of decisions; created by a will, for a purpose, to convey a message to an audience" (55). The contextual approach, when applied to photographs, demonstrates that they, like conventional textual records, "are documents created by a will, for a purpose, to convey a message to an audience" and that an understanding of their context "transforms photographic images into archival documents" (Schwartz 1995, 42).

One way to do this is through the application of diplomatics. Diplomatics is "the study of the creation, form, and transmission of records, and their relationship to the facts represented in them and to their creator, in order to identify, evaluate, and communicate their nature and authenticity" through "refined notions of what constitutes authority, authenticity, purpose, and the extrinsic and intrinsic elements" of the record (Pearce-Moses 2005; Bartlett 1996, 488). Diplomatics applied to historical photographs may "provide elasticity as well as rigor to both professional research and application by archivists" (Bartlett 1996, 486). Diplomatics encourages the identification of context, authorship, intentionality, and audience, since "rules of cultural and technical production do govern their creation" (Schwartz 1995, 57). By shifting from the content to the context of the photograph, "diplomatics has the potential to shed new light on both informational *and* evidential value and thus increase visual literacy" (Schwartz 1995, 42).

Photography in context

Culturally, there is an increasing awareness of the value of photography. An escalating demand for images makes new users seek photography more readily than ever before. Cultural heritage institutions hold an eclectic collection of historical and modern photography in which can be found the answers to an astonishingly wide range of questions. Through a contextual approach, information professionals can provide both intellectual and physical access to the images in response to these new demands.

Batchen (2008) states that "Photography's peculiarities—its faithful replication of what it sees, its simultaneous articulation of past, present, and future, its capacity for endless reproduction and shifting of shape, the infinite number of its projects—represent a seemingly insoluble historiographic challenge" (76). However, information professionals must accept this challenge, striving to document the visual record's rich contextual relationships, variety of narratives, and multi-provenancial characteristics.

Placing photography within context creates possibilities "to challenge existing interpretations and raise new questions, to weave the fabric of history in more elaborate patterns and color it in deeper hues" (Mifflin 2007, 65). For information professionals, context provides new ways of understanding photographs, documenting relationships, engaging users, and presenting images to the public.

Intellectual property rights

Copyright is the aspect of intellectual property that defines the rights of content producers and content consumers. Other aspects of intellectual property, such as patents and trademarks, are generally not applicable, because most cultural heritage institutions focus on literary and artistic works as they are defined in most national and international laws: written works (literary and otherwise), graphical works such as photographs, artistic works in other media, audio recordings, and film, video, and television.

Copyright is intended as a limited monopoly permitting authors to profit from their creative efforts and, eventually, allowing the public to freely use creative works, with the idea that such usage will inspire new creations that will benefit society. When a creative work is not subject to copyright protection, it is referred to as being in the public domain.

'Fair use' is a concept unique to United States law that provides a defense of copyright infringement in certain special situations. Fair use allows one to copy an otherwise protected work without the permission of the copyright owner and without the use being deemed an infringement. Other countries, such as the United Kingdom, have a similar concept called 'fair dealing,' but it is generally more restrictive. Fair use developed

Box 3.2   **Best practices for securing copyright**

- Possession of a physical item does not imply ownership of the copyright.
- The absence of a copyright notice does not mean the absence of copyright protection, particularly for newer or unpublished works.
- Factor in enough time to clear copyright, usually months.
- Assume, unless told otherwise, that a payment will have to be made in order to use copyrighted images.
- A letter of inquiry to the rights holder should outline the project, its potential audiences and uses, how long the images will be available, and the mode of distribution.
- Emphasize the academic, non-profit nature of the project.
- Try to cover all the instances in which the images may be used, so as to save time in reapplying for rights in the future.
- Stress the ways in which copyright will be protected, such as watermarking or password protection.
- Create a policy on image access and usage within the completed digital project, including, if appropriate, provision of copyright disclaimer forms.
- It may be necessary to negotiate the rate suggested by the copyright holder if the fee they suggest seems unreasonable.
- If you have identified a large collection that the project would like to use, approach the holding institution with the suggestion of becoming joint partners in the project.
- Keep a record of all correspondences and attempts to clear copyright in a diligence file.
- Agreements should be recorded in writing.
- Do not publish images if you have no record of permission to do so from the copyright holder; no response from the holder does not imply permission for use of the images.
- Consult the following websites for information on country-specific laws:

Box 3.2 Best practices for securing copyright (*Cont'd*)

Australia: National Library of Australia: Intellectual Property Rights Management:

www.nla.gov.au/padi/topics/28.html

Canada: Copyright Policy Branch:

www.pch.gc.ca/eng/1268266866591/1268268847192

International: World Intellectual Property Organization:

www.wipo.int/portal/index.html.en

United Kingdom: Intellectual Property Office: www.ipo.gov.uk/

United States: U.S. Copyright Office, Library of Congress:

www.copyright.gov/

---

as an equitable way of dealing with certain kinds of copying that, under specific circumstances, were deemed excusable for reasons of public policy. Fair use is available for only limited uses: for such purposes as criticism, comment, news reporting, teaching (including multiple copies for classroom use), scholarship, and research.

Rights management has major implications for image collections, especially for digitization initiatives. Most institutions select for digitization either photographs in which they own copyright or images that have passed into the public domain. Depending on the resources available, some institutions may wish to either secure copyright for the images in their care or investigate copyright, if the rights are unknown. However, this is a time-consuming and expensive process. If permissions are not forthcoming for copyrighted sources, the materials cannot be reproduced and the focus of the project must change. If there is limited means for copyright investigation, information professionals should concentrate on items of which the rights are owned by the institution. Additionally, from a risk management perspective, eliminating materials that are or may be under copyright will nullify the danger of infringement.

Once digital images are made available online, the organization hosting them should protect its rights. Copyright and legal issues are exacerbated by the openness and ubiquity of the internet. The potential for unauthorized and unlimited use of online materials means that access cannot be managed as carefully as in a traditional setting, where access restrictions allow sensitive materials to be presented with commentary, background materials, and guidance.

Access, when not universal, must be managed through passwords, user fees, or other means. Diverse capabilities for viewing, downloading, and printing may be offered to different sets of users. The simplest method of protection is for the delivery medium to carry a copyright statement and guidelines about the usage of the images. For example, on a website, the user would have to agree to abide by certain rules before viewing the images. Access could also be limited to registered users or users logging on from the institution's domain name or IP address. Additionally, institutions can insert captions, add watermarks to the images, or encrypt them.

Copyright and image-protection decisions must be made at the institutional level. Information managers should have access to training and up-to-date information and should always keep accurate, comprehensive documentation about all legal matters relating to their image collections. The presentation of material on the internet is inherently international, so information professionals should be aware of the wider context of global access and use of materials online. It is worthwhile, especially with a large digitization project, to obtain legal advice concerning copyright, as the law varies considerably internationally and, due to its complexity, is beyond the scope of this book.

Legal and cultural considerations

Information professionals should also be aware of other areas of concern that are not guided by codes of practice. Additionally, different international laws apply to these problematic categories.

Information professionals must proceed with caution regarding culturally sensitive content in relation to anthropological images, materials related to Native American communities or heritage, or any type of cultural property. Additionally, with materials that involve people photographed against their will or in exploitative situations, information professionals should be sensitive to the context of how the images were both captured and collected and consider the manner in which they will present such content.

The right of publicity generally is associated with public figures. Publicity rights address commercial gain from one's name, likeness, voice, persona, or other commercially exploited aspects of personality. Laws vary internationally, and in the United States, state by state. A further complication is that in some regions this right may continue after death, but in others ends upon the death of the subject.

The right of privacy relates to private citizens rather than celebrities, though there are significant exceptions. Also, in contrast to publicity rights, privacy rights are noncommercial in nature and protect people from intrusion into their private affairs, from the public disclosure of private information and from being presented in a false light. If the materials are sufficiently intrusive or embarrassing, the likelihood of obtaining permission from the subject is slim. The right of privacy generally ends upon the death of the subject. Each organization will have a different comfort level with the potential for controversy created by distributing images that could be perceived as violating privacy.

Images may have donor restrictions, or limitations on access or use that have been stipulated by the individual or organization who donated the materials. The restrictions may require that the collection, or portions of the collection, be closed for a period of time or that a specific credit line be used if materials from the collection are exhibited or published.

Obscenity and pornography are such complex areas of law that one must tread carefully. Images including nudity, especially involving children, and any depiction of minors engaged in sexually explicit conduct are obviously problematic. There are ongoing efforts to control pornographic material distributed on the internet, particularly child pornography, as well as efforts to protect child users of the internet from materials that are more appropriate for an adult audience. It is important to follow legislative efforts in this area.

Ethics

Credibility problems arising from the manipulation of images have existed since the early days of photography. Despite this, photographs are assumed to be accurate representations of reality, unless it is patently obvious that they have been manipulated. Viewing image collections online cannot be a viable alternative to the reading room experience unless the integrity of the digital images can be assumed. There must be a presumption that an honest effort has been made to replicate the original image accurately, to the degree that the technological constraints allow.

Any manipulation of digital images should always be done on a copy of the unprocessed image data file. The original raw data file is the standard to which the final image can and should be compared. Any deliberate or unavoidable deviations, such as cropping, must be documented. Institutions should establish a code of ethics for the creation, manipulation, and distribution of files. If a policy is in place, it will help to authenticate image files and establish the institution as a credible source for historical materials. Information professionals must "grasp the way in which photography constructs an imaginary world and passes it off as reality" and protect photographs in their care from any manner of misrepresentation (Sekula 2003, 443).

Preservation

Digital images exist as data until they are rendered by application software, operating systems, and hardware platforms, making them vulnerable to format obsolescence and media decay. Ensuring the longevity of digital files is complicated and costly. Whereas analog photographs are still viewable if damaged, electronic images are unusable if the data has become corrupted.

Digital preservation typically centers on the choice of interim storage media, the life expectancy of a digital imaging system, and the planned migration of digital files to future systems while maintaining both the full functionality and the integrity of the original digital system. Conway (2000) states, "In the digital world, preservation is the creation of digital products worth maintaining over time" (18).

Howard (2008) notes that information professionals "need to concern ourselves with 'bit rot,' or the decay of information within a digital file; hardware, software, and format obsolescence; and server crashes and

---

Box 3.3   Best practices for digital image preservation

- Address long-term preservation concerns at the outset. Start the selection process by considering the issues involved in the long-term maintenance of the images.

- Store media—usually a gold Compact Disc-Recordable (CD-R)—in an appropriate off-site environment. A fireproof vault is ideal.

- Monitor and recopy data as necessary.

- Outline a migration strategy for transferring data across generations of technology.

- Anticipate and plan for future technological developments.

other disasters" (16). The growth of digital content has created critical preservation problems that cannot be resolved by traditional methods. As Kuny warned in 1998:

> We are moving into an era where much of what we know today, much of what is coded and written electronically, will be lost forever. We are, to my mind, living in the midst of digital Dark Ages; consequently, much as monks of times past, it falls to librarians and archivists to hold to the traditional which reveres history and the published heritage of our times.

Nearly a decade later, Hope observed:

> Our biggest fear is that we are deep in a dark age where all of the digital information is going to be lost.... The digital data put on the early internet is gone. We have archival digital masters, and there no longer exist machines that can read them. (As quoted in Baca and Tronzo 2006, 51)

Three fundamental preservation strategies are refreshment, emulation, and migration. These strategies are designed to preserve the integrity of digital objects and to maintain the ability for users to retrieve, display, and use them in the face of constantly changing technology.

Refreshing involves periodically moving a file from one physical storage medium to another in order to avoid the obsolescence or degradation of the storage medium. Because physical storage devices decay, and because technological changes make older storage devices inaccessible to new computers, some ongoing form of refreshing is likely to be necessary for years to come.

Migration periodically converts data from one hardware or software configuration to another, or from one generation of computer technology to a subsequent one, preserving the essential characteristics of the data. Migration will gradually bring files into a narrower variety of standard, contemporary file formats, as only a handful of file formats will 'win out' and continue to be used.

Emulation is similar to migration, but focuses on the application software rather than on the files containing the data. Emulation combines software and hardware to reproduce the essential characteristics of one computer to another, allowing programs designed for a particular environment to operate in a different one. Emulation requires the creation of emulators, programs that translate code and instructions between systems. The objective is that, under emulation, older data will run on contemporary computers.

A significant gap in digital records created in the late twentieth and early twenty-first centuries already exists, and the long-term preservation of digital objects is a challenge facing not only the information sector, but also society as a whole. Institutions, governments, and national and international organizations are developing initiatives aimed at the preservation of digital media. The success of these initiatives will depend largely on continuing dialog between all the parties involved.

4

Photographic image collection management

Abstract: The increased use of photographs by scholars as legitimate sources of historical information has compelled information professionals to re-evaluate their appraisal and collection development policies. Appraisal of photographs is difficult to apply because of the unique nature of the medium, but it is essential that the same intellectual rigor applied to other historical textual records be adopted for visual records. This chapter explores image collection development since the late 1960s. A discussion of the importance of selection for analog and digital images and of developing appraisal criteria follows, emphasizing the importance of good selection techniques to ensure that resources are invested wisely. The chapter concludes with the selection of images for digital capture and conversion, a vital component of digitization initiatives.

Keywords: aesthetic values, collection development, evidential and informational values, image collections, intrinsic and artifactual values, photographic appraisal

A photograph is not a painting, a poem, a symphony, a dance. It is not just a pretty picture, not an exercise in contortionist techniques and sheer print quality. It is or should be a significant document, a penetrating statement, which can be described in a very simple term—selectivity. (Berenice Abbott, 1966)

Photography is a system of visual editing ... It is a matter of choosing from among given possibilities, but in the case of photography the number of possibilities is not finite but infinite. (John Szarkowski, 1966)

Photographs bear witness to a human choice being exercised in a given situation. A photograph is a result of the photographer's decision that it is worth recording that this particular event or this particular object has been seen. If everything there existed were continually being photographed, every photograph would become meaningless. (John Berger, 1972)

Introduction

In *The Photographer's Eye*, historian John Szarkowski (1966) writes, "The central act of photography, the act of choosing and eliminating, forces a concentration on the picture edge—the line that separates in from out" (9). Like photography itself, the selection of images to include in a visual collection or digitization project is a skilled process of selecting from among an unlimited number of options. Appraisal of photographs and other visual materials has remained on the picture edge—the "margins of archivy"—because "the inherent subjectivity of appraisal is exacerbated by the emotional, impulsive qualities of photographs" (Schwartz 2002, 144; Ballard and Teakle 1991, 43). To preserve the usefulness and authenticity of photography's complex, versatile form of documentary evidence, information professionals must reposition themselves from the picture's edge to its center, examining values and criteria and considering the medium's unique attributes, while being mindful of ecumenical documentary concerns.

This chapter examines the development of image collections since 1960. More importantly, it explores selection criteria for today's hybrid collections of analog and digital images, as well as guidelines unique to digitization initiatives. While specific criteria inform decisions in every institution, information professionals must be aware of universal appraisal issues.

Image collections

Cultural heritage institutions collect only a small portion of the body of information created and disseminated over time. In the nineteenth and early twentieth centuries, the collections of most research organizations were shaped by the needs of their scholars, resulting in predominately textual holdings that were deep but not broad in coverage. Under the influence of the growth of higher education after World War II, collections became more standardized and wider in scope. Many libraries in large, research-oriented institutions began collecting in all areas covered by their academic departments so as to attract faculty and graduate students and provide on-site access to their users.

Museums and archives began to collect and display noteworthy photography collections. The Museum of Modern Art established its photography department in 1940, and the George Eastman House International Museum of Photography and Film was opened to the public in 1949. The International Center of Photography, the Center of Creative Photography at the University of Arizona, and the Women in Photography International Archive were established in 1974, 1975, and 1981 respectively.

By the late 1960s and early 1970s, photography, which had remained largely on the margins of fine-art consciousness, began to become more accepted by significant institutions, and this contributed to its cultural and artistic status. University programs in photography created an educated audience in the post-war world that expanded exponentially in the 1970s and 1980s. Concurrently, influential criticisms of photography were published, including John Berger's *Ways of Seeing* (1972), Susan Sontag's *On Photography* (1977), and Roland Barthes' *Image-Music-Text* (published in France in 1961 and translated into English in 1977).

During this time, the art world sought to revitalize itself by promoting the sale and collection of historical and contemporary photography. Galleries devoted to photography were opened, such as the Witkin Gallery in New York City in 1969 and the Photographers' Gallery in London in 1971, the year in which Sotheby's held its first photography auction. Following the lead of Magnum, founded in 1947, photography agencies such as Gamma and Sygma were founded in 1967 and 1973.

Along with prominent private collectors, the corporate world turned to collecting photography in the 1960s and 1970s. Chase Manhattan Bank, the Gilman Paper Company, Hallmark, Polaroid, and Seagram's held significant collections of photography, many of which have been donated to museums.

The number of photography exhibitions increased, first in the United States and then in Europe. Nonetheless, it was only in 1989, photography's sesquicentennial year, that the Royal Academy held its first photography exhibition. That same year, the Whitney Museum of American Art Biennial included only one photographer (Grundberg 1999). As late as 2003, the Tate Modern in London mounted its first major photography show (Wells 2009).

Since the 1970s, research methodology has shifted to a greater reliance on visual documents as the topics of literary, historical, and sociological research have broadened to include many phenomena that are not well documented in texts. Women's history, for example, relies on sources from a variety of disciplines and uses photographs to illustrate the history of domestic life, among a myriad of other subjects. Relatively new fields, such as environmental studies, rely on the inadvertent documentation of built and unbuilt environments that would not have been remarked upon in texts.

Archives, libraries, and museums, as institutions for the accumulation and classification of knowledge, found their ideal form in photography, which provides a rich store of historical images. Traditionally associated with analog formats, image collections are now considered in a much broader context because of the possibilities offered by digital technologies. It is rare to find an institution that does not utilize digital technology for collection management, regardless of its size. Conferences of national and international associations, such as the Museum Computer Network, Museum Documentation Association, and Visual Resources Association, regularly include sessions on image applications.

Initial efforts at building digital collections were fueled by the widespread, rapid growth of the internet. During the 1990s, significant advances in computer technology created a wide user base. The decade saw a significant improvement in the color quality and resolution of computer displays, a rapid increase in central processing unit (CPU) power, a substantial increase in storage capacity, and an improvement in network speed, as well as each generation of technology costing less than its predecessor. Image collections online have become an essential form of cultural organization and memory, and their power consists in their relational potential, the possibility of establishing multiple connections between images and constructing narratives about cultures.

Collections of digitized and born-digital images need to be of sufficient volume to create a corpus of research materials that makes access worthwhile. Critical mass is formed when a sufficient quantity of related items in a collection create a richer digital collection than do its analog originals. Technology has the transformative power to not only recreate a collection online but also give it new functionality. Without critical mass, none of the time savings or convenience inherent in web-based research can be fully realized. Comprehensiveness is the key to satisfying digital research needs.

Image collections also need to be meaningful to the communities of which they are a part. Wolf (2006) states, "creating a database *ex nihilo* is virtually always the best solution, as this path alone can guarantee that the final result will exactly mirror the needs of the institution, its faculty, and students" (25).

Terras (2008) notes, "Those producing digital versions of holdings for use by the general public had better keep abreast of how the general public are using imaging technologies outside memory institution's [*sic*] environments, if they want their own offerings to be well used" (159). Stvilia and Jörgensen (2009) suggest "studying the photo-collection practices of users of Flickr [to] better understand users' needs in using these collections and better align traditional information services and tools with those needs" (54). This is especially important because digital images online attract "new, non-traditional and remote users" (Matusiak 2006, 479). Understanding users and their requirements is essential because, as Fry (2007) writes, "the generic user of an image of Napoleon is well-served by Google searching; the specific art historical need is not" (18).

Appraisal defined

Good image management hinges on the ability to choose wisely from an almost unlimited number of images of varying value. Appraisal, in an archival context, identifies materials offered to an institution that have "sufficient value to be accessioned" into the institution's holdings, depending on the "records' provenance and content, their authenticity and reliability, their order and completeness, their condition and costs to preserve them, and their intrinsic value" (Pearce-Moses 2005). Appraisal is "the intellectual activity of weighing the relative value of records to decide which ones may be destroyed and why, and which ones must be kept and why," serving the research interests of the community over time (Craig 2004, 2). Appraisal evaluates what can be successfully preserved and made accessible, balancing a collection's enduring values and usefulness against care and management costs (Vogt-O'Connor 2006). While most people are familiar with the definition of appraisal referring to an estimation of an item's monetary worth or resale value, in the archival context, appraisal refers to a comprehensive assessment of the values, legal requirements, and usefulness of images for researchers.

Because the significance of records cannot be determined from a preliminary assessment, appraisal is usually conducted after acquisition. Appraisal requires careful deliberation, since decisions not to save unique documents are irrevocable. Selection is especially important for photo-graphic collections, because while the costs of maintaining collections in any format are expensive, the costs related to visual formats are even more so (Boles 2005).

Appraisal for digitization projects is obligatory, but dissimilar to that for analog images. "Selection of an item for digitization is re-selection, and the criteria for its digitization, or re-proposing, will be different from those for its acquisition" (Smith 2002, 12). In this book, the terms 'appraisal' and 'selection' are used interchangeably and refer to the initial selection for the image collections of analog, born-digital, and digitized images, as well as re-selection for digitization initiatives.

Photographic appraisal

Appraisal of photographs has traditionally been neglected and "based primarily on their content and artistic merit," not on the sophisticated reading needed to assess their complex connotations (Boles 2005, 132). As early as 1979, Taylor wrote that "non-textual material showed little evidence of a time series and obstinately resisted an original order between inclusive dates," and therefore, "photographs were long ignored as records in the archival sense" (419). Schlak (2008) asserts that archivists have uncritically applied textual models to visual materials because they have not developed their own image selection standards.

> Given the ubiquity of images in modern life and the apparent lamentable lack of visual literacy among archivists and librarians, it is not difficult to understand why little effort is made to reconsider the photograph as an entity at once more and less than the historical content it purports to represent. (86)

Information professionals have switched from acquiring photographs from the first fifty years of photography's invention to selecting only a fraction of photographs in the age of abundance. Leary (1985) writes:

> Photo archivists have developed an unusually strong impulse to avoid thinking about the need for selection. After all, we have told each other, the most urgent task is to save what remains of the early photographic legacy, a task which many institutions ignored until recently. The salvage of nineteenth-century photography will remain an important responsibility of photo archives for the foreseeable future. Increasingly, however, the enormous bulk of twentieth-century photography will force photo archivists to confront the necessity of appraisal.

Images "are not only voluminous and highly fugitive, but also demanding of tailored visual, rather than hand-me-down textual approaches" (Schwartz 2004, 109). Bartlett (1996) comments on the changing attitudes of photographic appraisal, noting that appraisal of analog images seemed "more static, measurable, and relatively easy to detect" than that of digital images. "Rather than simply invalidate photographic media as now archivally suspect, [information professionals] should instead attempt to assess all photographic media, past and present, with a greater sensitivity to their inherently transitory and multiple qualities" (488).

The appraisal of photographs depends on a number of factors, such as mission statements, acquisition criteria, and collecting strategies. Appraisal policies for photographs "should be flexible enough to accommodate changing definitions of historical value" and "encourage greater consistency, and ensure rationalization and accountability" (Ballard and Teakle 1991, 43–44).

To determine whether photographic accessions meet the institution's criteria, Ericson (1991) suggests that appraisers ask "*Why* should I save this?" and "Why should *I* save this?" (68). While the first question addresses the value of an item as evidence, the second queries the appropriateness of an item for a particular collection. That the material is worth preserving is not enough, it must also meet the goals of the institution (Greene 1998).

Photograph acquisitions should also have strong documentation and chain of custody, the legal and physical ownership of records that proves their authenticity. They should display a depth of subject matter, genres, and formats and be in reasonable condition and quantity (Vogt-O'Connor 2006). Thoughtful consideration should be given to photographs without captions or provenance; duplicated elsewhere; in need of significant preservation, research, or arrangement to be useful; that have permanent access or usage restrictions; or that are too costly to acquire or manage (Vogt-O'Connor 2006). After selection, the result should be a high-quality, "discrete, cohesive, and hopefully unique collection" that fulfills the research needs of the institution's users (Murphy 2003, 155).

Photographic appraisal criteria

During appraisal, information professionals must "assume a role more active than that of passive presenter and processor of [visual] documents" by applying their knowledge and judgment and conducting preliminary research (Mifflin 2007, 33). Information professionals:

> must have the time needed to study the fonds, its creator, the context of creation of the documents, and a working knowledge of the history of photography.... Effort invested in this preparation, in this research, can save considerable time in the processing of photographs. (Charbonneau 2005, 137–138)

Figure 4.1   Tintype

Note: The clipped corners of this tintype are common in pictures intended for insertion into a paper display case. In the original, the woman's cheeks are painted pink. Examination of her clothes may indicate what year this picture was taken. Dresses could be modified from year to year, but bonnets were more up to date because they were purchased more often.

Source: Tintype, recto, 3½ × 2½ in (8.9 × 6.4 cm). Author's collection.

In reviewing the pertinent criteria for the appraisal of photographs, Charbonneau (2005) determines that subject, quality, age, originality, documentation, aesthetics, and accessibility affect appraisal decisions. User needs and the intentions of the participants in the creation of photographs also contribute to the appraisal process. Participants include the photographer, the individual or group photographed, the customer or sponsor of the photography shoot, the technician, and the individual who gathers and documents the photographs.

The National Archives of Australia has developed specific criteria for photographic appraisal which include research value, cost, identifying information, quality, and quantity (Ballard and Teakle 1991). Research value usually depends upon the subject of the record, which is elevated if the subject is "essential to the interpretation or understanding of related records which have been appraised as having long-term value or [have] a high intrinsic value" (45). Subjects that influence research value include people, work, and social activities; objects; and natural phenomena; as well as known or important photographers. Cost also affects appraisal, with research value balanced against the expense of preservation. Identifying information encompasses subjects, dates, locations, individual names, and photographers; provenance often supplements missing information. Quality highlights the photograph's evidential, informational, aesthetic, intrinsic, and artifactual values, while quantity refers to uniqueness of the subjects depicted.

Aesthetic values

Cook (1980) believes that the separation and special treatment of photographs reduces information professionals to curators, judging artistic merit over traditional research values. Schwartz (1995) counters this:

> The pejorative tone attached to the term "curator" usually derives from the erroneous assumption that a photo-archivist is motivated by the same concerns as the curator, namely artistic merit or connoisseurship. But aesthetic considerations are a minor element of the archival appraisal of photographs.... Just as good grammar assists verbal communication and standardizes comprehension, aesthetic quality aids visual communication. (56)

Boles (2005) writes:

> many archivists likely have preserved images simply for their artistic merit. Artistic merit does matter. Perhaps the best way to think about the place of aesthetics in archival selection is to consider it a "visual grammar." Just as good grammar can make textual records easier to read and more effective, a well-composed

> picture makes the author's point more forcefully than a poorly framed image. The rules of composition, like the rules of grammar, improve the final product. (133)

To fulfill their historical research potential and to be reproducible for publications and exhibits, photographs should have "proper focus to render detail, exposure that preserves the full range of tonal contrast, clarity, satisfactory composition and be in good physical condition"—in short, be aesthetically appealing (Ballard and Teakle 1991, 47). Szarkowski (1966) notes that a photograph's aesthetics are derived from the interaction between "the thing itself" (the subject), the detail, the frame, time, and the vantage point. While these artistic characteristics contribute to composition, photographs used in historical research were taken and preserved for more prosaic reasons than art.

Evidential and informational values

Fraser (1981) notes that generally "photographs are not acquired and retained for their aesthetic value or intellectual content, but are expected to serve some useful purpose" (139). Among those most valuable to scholars are photographs that document people, places, things, and events for the purposes of reporting news, encouraging reform, advertising a product or service, promoting a government program, explaining a scientific or industrial process, or illustrating an idea. What are more significant than a photograph's aesthetics, especially during appraisal, are the image's evidential and informational values as confirmation of its creator's activities and its subjects.

Regarding archival appraisal, Schellenberg (1965) distinguishes between primary and secondary values. Primary values are those immediate to the creation of the record, its original administrative, legal, or fiscal purpose for its creators. After their first purpose, records can also acquire secondary values for historical research—their evidential and informational values, which are not mutually exclusive. Evidential values reflect the importance of records as evidence of the organization, its functions, its policies, and the operations of the records creator, for accountability and historical purposes rather than legal purposes. Informational value relates to any other uses of records for documentation of society or historical information, providing unique and permanent information for the purposes of research.

Traditionally, photographs have been generally valued for their informational content. Schellenberg (1965) writes:

Information on the provenance of pictorial records within some government agency, corporate body, or person is relatively unimportant, for such records do not derive much of their meaning from their organizational origins.... Information on the functional origins of pictorial records is also relatively unimportant. (325)

Leary (1985) asserts that photographs:

possess minimal evidential value. Frequently, photographs provide some evidence of an organization's operation, but written records are almost always a better source of essential evidential values.... Photographs that show official activities and nothing else are likely to be very boring and insignificant images.

Charbonneau (2005) agrees, noting that photographs require different appraisal models than textual records:

Photographs are distinct from textual documents in that their most important value is informational. This means that archivists cannot resort to their traditional methods when beginning an appraisal for the selection of photographs; that is to say the assessment of the evidential value of the documents which reflects their bond with the creator of the fonds. (120)

The prevailing notion that photographs can only be appraised for their informational values may have developed because their evidential values have been obscured, weakened, or destroyed during acquisition and processing. When photographs are removed from their provenance and original order, the informational value is the only quality that remains intact.

Evidential values are derived from the context of creation, original and subsequent use, preservation history, authorship, purpose, message, and audience. In order to understand evidential values, information professionals must "abandon their faith in the function of the photographic document as a truthful representation of material reality and cease to equate archival value with image content" (Schwartz 1995, 46). Further, "by embracing a textual model of recorded information ... archives continue to fixate on the factual content rather than the functional origins of visual images" (Schwartz 2002, 143). Ballard and Teakle (1991) note that the interpretation of photographs engages information professionals at a "complex cognitive [sic] level that is

Figure 4.2 **Cabinet card, front and back**

(a)

(b)

Note: The ornate illustrations on the front and back of this cabinet card provide clues about the image, such as the image's date (after 1889, because of the copyright notice) and the photographer's name and location.

Source: Albumen print cabinet card, recto and verso, 6½ × 4¼ in (16.5 × 10.8 cm). Author's collection.

culturally based. The aim is to recognize the original intention of the photograph—its particular cultural use by particular people. This is rarely given within the picture but is developed in its function or context" (44). Photographs with "intact original arrangement by the creator are useful as they allow repository staff to infer information from the context and to assume the authenticity and judge the reliability of the accession" (Vogt-O'Connor 2006, 78). Kaplan and Mifflin (2000) add, "photographers' notes and other complementary sources should be sought out, preserved, and made available" (121). Schwartz (1995) asserts that "archival value in photographs resides in the interrelationship between photographs and the creating structures, animating functions, programmes and information technology that created them" (50). Sassoon (2007) affirms:

Photographs are complex, multilayered objects whose archival values derive from series of interrelationships between photographs and other archival formats, and the dynamics between what is visible and what is invisible. What is invisible are the ephemeral, provenance-based relationships from which archives in original order gain their authenticity, and where viewing serial relationships provides evidence of the broader warps and wefts which are inaccessible when seeing a single thread. (139)

Unfortunately, these interrelationships are often lost during preservation because evidential value is

embedded in the physical structure of the album, its sequence of pages, the placement of images, the juxtaposition of words and images, and the larger documentary universe of which it is a part is sacrificed in a misguided effort to ensure the long-term physical stability of individual photographs. The meaning of the album, not simply as a housing for the images, but as a document in its own right, and the information it was compiled to communicate is lost. (Schwartz 2002, 157)

Additionally, digitization may also obliterate evidential value. Westney (2007) warns that "the major risk posed by digital surrogates is the loss of evidential value due to the destruction of evidence as to the context and circumstances of their origin" (7). Sassoon (2007) writes:

Seduced by both the subject content and visual qualities of photographic archives, and the ease of access that digitisation technology affords, archivists are overseeing the erosion of the transactional nature of records and core principles of archival practice.... What has emerged in this new electronic environment is a digital domain with orphans of archivists' own creation. What have been liberated through technology in the 21st century are archival principles. (139)

Viewing photographs with their archival provenance and original order intact makes determining evidential values possible, providing "a hedge against error, discouraging the superimposition of meanings" (Mifflin 2007, 34).

Intrinsic and artifactual values

Beyond evidential and informational values, intrinsic and artifactual values should also be appraised. Intrinsic value is the significance of an item derived from its physical or associational qualities (based on its relationship to an individual, family, organization, place, or event), inherent in its original form and generally independent of its informational or evidential value. Artifactual value is the significance of an item based on its physical or aesthetic characteristics, rather than its intellectual content. Schwartz (2002) notes that a daguerreotype as an artifact tells users just as much as does the image it captures:

> The word "daguerreotype" for example indicates far more than process. It immediately narrows the date of the document to the twenty-year period of the 1840s and 1850s; it indicates that the photograph is a unique image which was produced using certain kinds of apparatus and refractory procedures; it indicates that, as a form of photograph, it circulated in certain ways and followed certain trajectories, that it was never tucked into a report or glued into an album, that [it] is unlikely to bear a handwritten inscription, and that it must be understood, in part, from its social life as a thing and its materiality as an object. (154)

Figure 4.3 Cased tintype, front and back

(a) (b)

Note: This hand-colored tintype is cased in glass and foil to resemble the more expensive ambrotype. It can easily fit in the palm of the hand for private viewing, and functions as an artifact of material culture.

Source: Tintype, recto and verso detail, 2½ × 2 in (6.4 × 5.1 cm). Author's collection.

Records with intrinsic value have qualities that make their original physical form "the only archivally acceptable form for preservation" (Westney 2007, 6). These characteristics may include aesthetic quality, content, usage, market value, unique physical features, age, or scarcity. Vogt-O'Connor (2006) writes that images with strong artifactual and informational or evidential values are:

> by far the most heavily used images in most repositories. High artifactual value is what historians, teachers, and students, as well as curators, designers, exhibit curators, filmmakers, publishers, and web designers, look for in photographs, particularly for images to reproduce, exhibit, or publish. (126)

Intrinsic and artifactual values determine whether photographs should receive conservation treatment in their original format or should be reformatted as copies, and if special security or access protections are needed (Vogt-O'Connor 2006).

Selection for digitization

The development of selection policies is a core component of digital projects, and numerous selection guidelines and criteria have been developed by institutions, national governments, and international organizations. Hazen et al. (1998) state:

> The process of deciding what to digitize anticipates all the major stages of project implementation. Digital resources depend on the nature and importance of the original source materials, but also on the nature and quality of the digitizing process itself—on how well relevant information is captured from the original, and then on how the digital data are organized, indexed, delivered to users, and maintained over time.

Institutions need to validate their selection procedures for digitization with reference to external criteria, especially with the increase of collaboration for digital projects. Additionally, funding is most likely to be available where proposed digitization programs meet agreed criteria in terms of preparation, selection, and image capture. Hazen et al. (1998) advise that institutions:

Figure 4.4 **Selection flowchart**

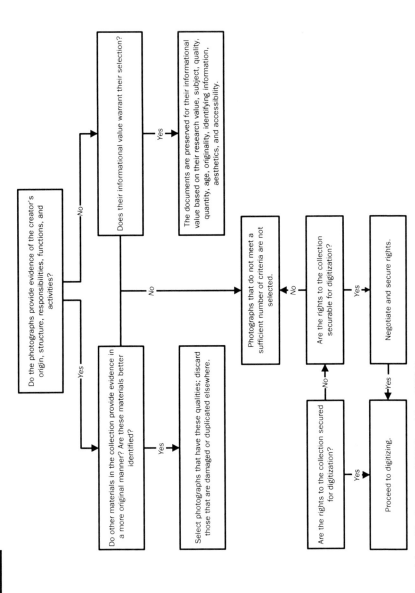

The photographs provide evidence of the creator's origin, structure, responsibilities, functions, and activities?

No → Does their informational value warrant their selection?

Yes → The documents are preserved for their informational value based on their research value, subject, quality, quantity, age, originality, identifying information, aesthetics, and accessibility.

Yes → Do other materials in the collection provide evidence in a more original manner? Are these materials better identified?

Yes → Select photographs that have these qualities; discard those that are damaged or duplicated elsewhere.

No → Photographs that do not meet a sufficient number of criteria are not selected.

No → Are the rights to the collection securable for digitization?

Yes → Negotiate and secure rights.

Are the rights to the collection secured for digitization?

Yes → Proceed to digitizing.

Yes → Proceed to digitizing.

No →

Source: Adapted from Charbonneau (2005) and Lee (2001).

place the questions of what and how to digitize into the larger framework of collection building by focusing, first, on the nature of the collections and their use, and, second, on the realities of the institutional context in which these decisions are made.

Since only a small percentage of an image collection can be digitized, information professionals must determine what is most worthwhile to convert. Selection should be influenced by the previously mentioned criteria of aesthetic, evidential, informational, intrinsic, and artifactual values, as well as indicators unique to the digital realm.

The most important selection criterion for digitization is the copyright status of the original materials. The copyright of images should be held by the organization or be in the public domain. If not, permission to digitize must be obtained from the rights holder. If the institution does not have the right to digitize, then other images must be chosen, otherwise the project cannot proceed.

Issues regarding intellectual property, cultural sensitivities, privacy and publicity rights, obscenity, and pornography, if not dealt with properly, can lead to lawsuits and costly settlements. Additionally, donor restrictions must be investigated so as to determine whether the images can be digitally captured and presented online. Digitization performed without thoughtful selection may result in the creation of digital files that cannot be effectively used, due to legal restrictions. Determining the legal status of candidate materials is a crucial step in any digital selection process. If institutions have images that are encumbered by an onerous permissions process, it may be more expeditious to consider other collections for digitization.

Usage is another factor which determines a collection's priority for digitization. Ayris (1998) states:

> There is no point in selecting materials for digitization if there is no support for using the resource amongst target user groups. This tenet is identical to guidance in a conventional collection development policy. No paper material would be purchased by a library if potential use could not be identified amongst library users.

The images selected should support current prioritized activities, public programs, and outreach activities, such as exhibitions, publications, and cultural events; should enhance the strengths of the institution; and should have potential for enduring value as digital objects. Items with a pedagogical utility for classroom use, curriculum support, or distance education are also ideal for digitization.

If analog images are well used, researchers will most likely also be interested in their digitized versions. Conversely, underused images may be good candidates for digitization if they are of broad interest and a realistic expectation exists for attracting new users. Discussing the digitization of the special collections of the University of the Pacific, Sutton (2008) provides the following example:

> In selecting materials for digitization, there was an overarching goal of including both well-known and underutilized collections that could be integrated into the University's curriculum. The most prominent collections in Special Collections are the papers of naturalist John Muir and jazz musician Dave Brubeck. Since these are also the two most heavily used collections, inclusion of their content was a priority. At the same time, digitization offered opportunities to increase awareness and use of other significant but lesser-known materials. A prime example is the nineteenth-century diaries of Delia Locke, the wife of a rural doctor and rancher in northern California. While Locke is not a famous Californian, her diaries provide a unique perspective on California history, now accessible to a much wider audience through digitization. These diaries were also chosen because of their relevance to several academic disciplines including history, women's studies, and religious studies. (29)

However, images selected for conversion and hosted online, even if they are highly used in analog form, are only a subset of the whole collection. Online aggregations of images give the public access to an edited view of history, rather than the more balanced perspective they would have if they were aware of the context from which the photographs originated. Sassoon (2007) warns:

> The digitising process and the viewing technology encourages a focus on content, and this can lead to pressure for individual items to be selected more for their aesthetic content than their archival values. Through their own actions (albeit at times under pressure), archivists are active in replacing the original narrative of production with new institutional "narratives of luck" born in the digital domain. Through this, and where images are posted on websites as single items without reference to context or presentational form, digitisation is creating a databank of orphans which have been removed from their transactional origins and evidence of authorial intent. (139)

Although making selection decisions on the basis of use is tenable, doing so limits search results to repeated use of the same images, perhaps without proper context. Information professionals must determine the sapient balance between digitizing popular images and providing a richer representation of the institution's holdings.

Potential projects should be evaluated as to whether appropriate intellectual control can be provided for the original images and their digital surrogates. Information professionals should assess the degree to which the images are arranged in a way suited to online use; whether cataloging, processing, and related organizational work is already accomplished; and whether there are appropriate staff and resources to support the creation of metadata related to image identification.

Selected images should also be considered for the technical feasibility of digitization. The degree to which a digital version can represent the full content of the original, whether the images will display well digitally, and the capacity for accessing images from current institutionally supported platforms and networked environments and delivering them with reasonable speed are factors to consider. The images should be at least as easy to use digitally as in their original form and should allow for improved access and new types of utilization when digitized.

Images that have restricted access, due to their condition, value, vulnerability, or location should be considered for digitization so that access to originals can be reduced for preservation and safety purposes. Additionally, some images or collections may be chosen so as to enhance image quality. Digital conversion provides high-quality surrogates which, in most cases, will both protect the original images from handling and satisfy users of today and tomorrow.

Collections of images may be selected for digitization because of requests from potential partners in collaborative or consortial efforts. Digital conversion encourages new usage between organizations, and collections that are split among a number of institutions can be united online. Research may be enhanced by integrating images that otherwise would have remained separated in different parts of the world. The flexible integration and synthesis of a variety of formats, of related materials scattered among many locations, and the contribution to the development of a critical mass of digital images in subject areas should also be considered.

To make a digitization project worthwhile requires a certain minimum volume of information. Otherwise, the research value will be too low to attract a sufficient number of planned or potential users. An important consideration is whether an entire collection or a part of it will be digitized. The value of photographs is higher in aggregate, rather than as single items taken out of context.

Other criteria include an examination of the strategic motives for initiating digitization projects, the institutional framework that will support them, and funding opportunities. Whatever the factors behind the decision to convert images to digital format, the selection process will be further refined along a continuum that will require reassessment in successive stages.

Managing hybrid collections

Digital technology is a valuable instrument to enhance learning and extend the reach of information resources. Digital information changes the way heritage institutions function and, more fundamentally, the work that they do. There is no doubt that digitization enables much broader access to cultural heritage collections and that increased access serves many functions, from education to entertainment. Evidence demonstrates that both traditional and non-traditional audiences can leverage the power of online access and use worldwide cultural heritage collections in innovative and unexpected ways. Furthermore, given the current state of analog media deterioration, creating surrogate copies of a heritage collection is a far better alternative than losing documentary evidence of that heritage.

For information professionals managing hybrid collections of analog, digitized, and born-digital images, selection is an indispensable tool to create online collections with global access and usage. No diktats regulate appraisal, only selection criteria to provide guidance within the context of the individual institution. When information professionals apply their knowledge and judgment to a general set of selection criteria and principles, matching image collections to their institutional goals and priorities, the result should be a visual representation of history with enduring value.

5

Metadata and information management

Abstract: Information professionals have traditionally assisted users in defining and expressing their image needs and helped them match those needs to images. These requests are often challenging to satisfy, due to the disconnection between the words users employ and the attributes used in systems for image retrieval. Image collections must be supported by a robust metadata structure that can accommodate and preserve a variety of discipline-specific metadata while supporting consistent access across collections, but metadata creation is one of the most expensive components of digital projects. This chapter investigates the challenges of image description, both at the item and collection level and considerations for subject description; it also explores the practical and philosophical challenges posed by the indexing aspect of image metadata construction, summarizes current practices, and outlines the factors that influence decisions about metadata created for digital content.

Keywords: content representation, Dublin Core, MARC, metadata, standards, subject description

> We want to describe the indescribable: nature's instantaneous text. We have lost the art of describing the only reality whose structure lends itself to poetic representation: impulses, aims, oscillations. (Osip E. Mandelstam, 1933)

> Ein Bild sagt mehr als 1000 Worte. [A picture says more than a thousand words.] (Kurt Tucholsky)

> A photograph is a secret about a secret. The more it tells you, the less you know. (Diane Arbus)

Introduction

In July 1945, *Atlantic Monthly* published "As We May Think," by army scientist Vannevar Bush, an essay that had an immense influence on the history of computing. Bush was concerned that "the summation of human experience is being expanded at a prodigious rate, and the means we use for threading through the consequent maze to the momentarily important item is the same as was used in the days of square-rigged ships." The article described a device called a Memex, an intuitive, associative retrieval system designed to supplement memory. Bush envisioned a desk with screens that would allow users to view documents, add notes, and create associations through a body of work using microfilm. The Memex was a conceptual ancestor to electronically linked materials and, ultimately, the internet. Bush's ideas were expanded by Theodor Nelson, who, in 1961, coined the terms 'hypertext' and 'hypermedia' to describe an environment in which text, images, and video could be digitally interconnected.

The popularity of the internet and the improvement of technology allowed for online access to images, and created an impetus for many institutions to provide deeper descriptive information for their visual holdings (Kaplan and Mifflin 2000). Image collections are among the least accessible resources available because of their size, organization, physical fragility, and rudimentary cataloging. Many collections consist of large groups of related materials that share one or more significant characteristics, such as source, subject, or medium.

Institutions that require access to large collections rely upon online image databases, but information professionals face problems of sheer magnitude when dealing with image collection growth of an unprecedented scale. Turner (1993) states, "A large mass of visual documents has now accumulated, and those responsible for acquiring, conserving, and providing access to images are faced with many serious problems. Not the least of these problems is providing subject access to these images" (241). Information professionals wish to increase the number of access points to the photographs in their care so as to help users navigate through the collection more efficiently. This chapter explores the challenges of describing image collections, summarizes current practices, and outlines the factors that influence decisions about creating metadata for digital content.

Description for archives, libraries, and museums

Description of images has sought to combine traditional library and archival practices with the more focused descriptive practices found in the museum and visual resources communities. Libraries catalog published, non-unique items, such as books and serials, which are produced in multiple copies and have a list of objective descriptors, such as author, title, publisher, and year, that appear printed in the book and leave little room for subjective opinion. As soon as one library catalogs a book, any library can copy that cataloging and apply it to its holdings. Catalogers in libraries use standards such as MARC (Machine-Readable Cataloging) and AACR2 (Anglo-American Cataloging Rules, Second Edition) with LCSH (Library of Congress Subject Headings) descriptors. AACR2 and MARC are heavily biased toward printed documents, which is not surprising, given that these standards matured before digital assets became commonplace. Libraries have begun to catalog individual images in their collections only since the 1980s, but have typically not described the collections that contain them.

Museums, on the other hand, have acquired great expertise in describing their unique holdings, usually describing the collection first and the individual items second, grouping items by artist, media, provenance, or historical period. Description often includes style or genre, history and use of the item, and preservation details. Much of the information registered when cataloging an artwork at one museum cannot be copied and applied to another work held by another institution. The attributes of the items and their most basic descriptors are often speculative or subjective. For example, artist name, year of production, and place of origin do not appear alongside the work at its creation, as in a book, but rather require curators to research them and come to their own conclusions. This subjective method of description can lead to different information about the same object in cases where multiple copies are held by different institutions. Practices also vary because of the diverse nature of individual museums and their collections.

Archives create detailed descriptions of unique materials or their surrogate representations, usually original unpublished material or primary sources, which can be expressed at both item and collection level. In archival practice, description expands upon information gleaned during the appraisal and arrangement of a collection, a process which produces preliminary descriptive forms such as container lists, summarizes the context and content of archival materials at multiple levels, and adds usage restrictions and access points for creators and subjects (Zinkham 2006). Archives catalog their materials using a combination of subjective descriptive texts and individual cataloging fields.

Challenges of image description

Visual collections often do not have a clearly defined or pre-existing organizational structure, individual titles, or creator names by which they can be described (Ritzenthaler and Vogt-O'Connor 2006). In the case of libraries and archives, it was a natural progression for them to apply to the description of images the methods that they had already developed to describe books and documents. However, these bibliographic methods have not fully addressed the unique characteristics of image collections. No single description method has been developed that can meet the image description needs of all archives, libraries, and museums, and differences in their descriptive practices make searching for images across types of institutions difficult.

Cataloging images is "idiosyncratic, knowledge-intensive, and time-consuming," because "the very characteristics that make [images] valuable also make them difficult to describe" (Dannenbaum 2008, 16; Shatford 1984, 14). Poor-quality records often exist because they are "created by people who are not catalogers, are created based on local practice that does not facilitate interoperability, or are based on curatorial traditions that do not translate well" for managing images (Lytle 2006, 21–22). Norris (1985) states:

> The evolution of photography from an arcane and highly technical craft practiced by a few professionals to a popular pastime of millions and a standard tool for documenting news, science, and business has resulted in voluminous collections that render traditional graphic cataloging techniques inadequate if not obsolete. (129)

Adding to that difficulty, image description and retrieval is essentially an act of translation, complicated by transforming

> concepts and visual perceptions to words, especially to specialized terms that might appear in an index or thesaurus, and mapping the terms of a mental model or natural-language query to controlled language [which is] fundamentally different from the processes of subject cataloging of texts. (Woll 2005, 20)

Baca (2002) writes:

> Searching for images is perhaps even more problematic than searching for text-based resources, as users must rely on how well

the images are indexed with words if they can hope to retrieve them.... Anyone familiar with art information knows that often the subject matter or theme of a work of art is not reflected at all in its title. Hence if I want to quickly find images of "Family life in the nineteenth century" which could have an infinite variety of titles, I can only find them if the descriptive terms "family life" and "nineteenth century" have been applied to them by a human being who has looked at an image, interpreted the file, the visual information, and other available data, and made the decision to apply these data values to it. (134)

Even with the emergence of online catalogs, web-accessible collections, and improved information searching and navigation, access to visual collections has remained limited, due to a lack of standardized description and integrated modes of access. Lytle (2006) notes, "There is need for more tools to automate processes for metadata creation, revision, and harvesting [which would] provide benefits in terms of consistency, interoperability, and long-term viability of meaningful metadata" (17). He continues:

> The initial expense and difficulty of creating high-quality metadata is compounded by the need for constant revision to correct mistakes and incorporate revisions to subject terms, taxonomies, and controlled vocabularies, along with revisions to meet the continually evolving patron research needs. (26)

Description presents information not otherwise provided on the images; photographs, whether analog or digital, often enter heritage institutions with little identification. Turner (1993) writes, "Because there is usually no text available ... success in retrieval is dependent on the surrogate which is created at the storage end to represent the image, and on the subjective judgment of the indexer" (249). Shatford (1986) asks:

> Rather than pretend that certain aspects of picture indexing are objective, would it not be better to admit that subjectivity exists, acknowledge its drawbacks (chiefly, that it leads to inconsistency) and recognize that subjective judgments and analysis can provide valuable access to information? (57)

"As long as a human element is involved in the cataloguing process—something that will remain with us for the foreseeable future—the role of the cataloguer is destined to be the most significant in the entire classification process" (Hourihane 2002). Deegan and Tanner (2002) state:

> The description of non-textual data in text is problematic as there is more room for subjectivity of perception on the part of the cataloger than with textual materials. Textual materials are often "self describing:" they contain textual information about subjects or keywords that can be extracted from the resource itself. With non-textual data, the metadata is created by individuals who, with the help of the range of reference works, make the most objective assessment possible about the object, but subjective bias is unconscious and cannot entirely be ruled out. (117)

De Polo and Minelli (2006) recapitulate:

> Some information is easily and immediately associated with pictures belonging to the archive, but most information needs research. A picture of an old man sitting on a chair, for example, has a different cultural value if one knows that the person portrayed is Théophile Gautier (a famous French author). (102)

Information about the images can be gleaned from whatever materials are available at the time of their acquisition. Thorough scrutiny of the images may reveal details from which to formulate descriptions. If the viewer is familiar with the subject matter of the unidentified image, it is possible to decipher signs, posters, numerals, advertisements, and other clues. Sometimes, research on the subject of the images can inform the work of description, although it should be confirmed from multiple sources.

For analog images, the chronology of the history of photography is another important tool for identifying photographs. An accurate knowledge of the periods during which specific photographic processes were used is significant, as many were in use for as little as three to four years.

Item-level description

Greene and Meissner (2005) found that "[f]rom the mid-1960s to the present, [information professionals in their writings] have dismissed arrangement at the item level as having little utility and being thoroughly impractical for modern collections" (213). Despite the literature, Greene and Meissner's repository and grant proposal surveys found that a large proportion of archivists have adhered to item-level description, even though it is contrary to the traditional archival practice of collection-level description. The same discrepancy between literature and practice appears to be true for the description of visual collections.

Item-level description is more common with visual materials than with textual materials. "Conventional processing techniques for pictorial collections presuppose that photographs must be treated individually" (Norris 1985, 129). Information professionals must evaluate their visual collections in order to determine if item-level description is warranted. Critics such as Dooley (1995) call item-level description of visual materials "insupportably expensive and unnecessary" and a "relic of a more leisurely past" (88). Schwartz (2002) notes that it is difficult to apply traditional description to visual materials:

> Traditional item-level description of photographs, indexed by subject and credited to the photographer, but without adequate contextual information about their functional origins and provenance, or clear links to such contextual information, transforms photographic archives into stock photo libraries, reducing photographs to their visible elements, and conflating photographic content and photographic meaning. (157)

Moir (1993) argues, "The diverse array of information that can appear within a single photographic image suggests that the most effective access is provided through description at the item level, in spite of the overwhelming strain on financial and human resources that such an approach entails" (75). Although it is time consuming, item-level description makes images searchable, and, with digital surrogates, viewable without having to retrieve the originals. However, resources are seldom adequate to catalog all collections to item level, and item-level handling should exist within a framework provided by group-level description. Repositories with limited budgets may digitize one or two representative images, while noting that there are additional, unscanned images (Ritzenthaler and Vogt-O'Connor 2006).

Ideally, an adequate amount of information should be provided for each image. In addition, the image should be searchable by subject, through subject headings or keywords. Item-level records tagged with keywords can provide the most information and are the most searchable, both within and among collections. However, due to the labor involved, labelling images with keywords may be impractical for sustained digitizing initiatives with collections of any significant size.

Box 5.1   Possible descriptors for image collections

- Titles of the collection or images.

- Names of the persons or organizations who created, accumulated, or maintained the images, including variant names and pseudonyms.

- Subjects or themes.

- Functions, activities, or roles for which the images were created, used, and assembled.

- Date(s) of creation.

- Geographic terms identifying place names or physical features.

- Relationships with other organizations or persons.

- Quantity or extent.

- Formats.

- Size.

Source: Adapted from Roe (2005).

Collection-level description

Although some information professionals debate the necessity for item-level access, it is often more difficult to describe images in the aggregate. Collection-level description can be useful for images of the same subject, but problematic for collections with a variety of subjects, as it neither improves retrieval nor limits handling of the originals. Ritzenthaler and Vogt-O'Connor (2006) agree that group arrangement and description are necessary and acceptable for large photograph collections or when resources are limited. Norris (1985), in his case study of two very large photograph processing projects, states of description at the group or collection level that "something is better than nothing" (133).

Collections can be accessed as single units or organized intellectually under a single classification while being physically stored or electronically displayed in separate groupings. Collections tend to be characterized by a coherence that binds the contents together and, as a result, totality enhances the research value of each individual item beyond what it would have in isolation.

Alexander and Meehleib (2001) note that the Library of Congress, Prints and Photographs Division (P&P) catalogers employ practices from libraries, museums, and archives. They evaluate the appropriate descriptive treatment for a given group of materials: whether the images should be cataloged at the item, group, or collection level. P&P catalogers create catalog records and finding aids frequently using a combination of description levels to facilitate access. This blended approach allows control over holdings at the group level as well as specific control over individual images at item level. This is especially important for high-demand images, images used in exhibits, or images with high intrinsic or market value. Although P&P represents a large image holding with vast resources, this example demonstrates that evaluative methods can determine the level of description required.

Subject description

The literature about subject indexing of images emphasizes the need for greater access at the pre-iconographical or primary subject level of description. Description generally concerns an image's secondary subject matter. This means that a patron must have a certain amount of specialized knowledge in order to find an image. Markey (1986) remarks, "Anyone searching a collection of visual images accessible [only] by secondary subject matter is at the mercy of the indexer's interpretation" (7). Additionally, one cannot search across a collection for basic attributes. Collins (1998) notes:

> Given the increasingly interdisciplinary nature of research, it is desirable that a collection of images be searchable by persons from any field and for a great variety of purposes. In many institutions, however, retrieving an image requires knowledge of its creator or of its title, supplied by either the image creator or the cataloger. Often, only collection-level descriptions are available. This means that image construct queries are simply not possible, and the patron must either have specialized subject knowledge or rely heavily on the memories of individual collection managers.... Describing images by their primary subject matter preserves information that both specialists and nonspecialists can use to gain access to the collection. (37, 40)

Keefe (1990) provides an example of how added subject headings for holdings of the Rensselaer Architecture Library's Slide Collection provided greater subject access for users:

> While the title (Sydney Opera House) is still the primary notation, the slide document itself also contains information on a variety of subjects (e.g., Ridge Beams, Glass Curtain Walls, Tiles, Shell Vaults, Precast Concrete Ribs, Concert Halls, etc.). These different references now make that slide available to those patrons needing examples of different types of materials, structures, and/or designs. It means that a slide of a statue in a fifteenth-century Gothic cathedral is now available to the student or professor of Medieval history who needs examples of armor or dress from the Middle Ages. Viewing a slide as a document instead of a composition significantly increases its usefulness as a visual resource (663).

Access to analog image collections is usually provided through finding aids which include subject indexing only for large collections, if at all. Studies indicate that, among a variety of libraries and archives, the most frequent approach to image retrieval is by subject (Armitage and Enser 1997). Tibbo (1993) found that with historical photograph collections, subject descriptors were by far the most commonly used terms, while words indicating place, time, and proper names were next in importance. Collins (1998) advises:

> Regardless of the time and expense involved, without subject access, many requests for images could not be answered. The fact that the overwhelming majority of the patrons ... sought images by subject indicates the importance of these terms for retrieval. Any amount of subject indexing, even of only the main subjects of photographs, could only improve access. (53)

Layne (1994) suggests that whatever the depth of subject description chosen for images:

> The indexing of images should accomplish two things: first, the indexing of images should provide access to images based on the attributes of those images; and second, the indexing of images should provide access to useful groupings of images, not simply access to individual images.... When devising indexing schemes or

indexing images, it is necessary to decide which attributes need to be indexed, which can be simply noted in conjunction with images, and which may be left for the searcher for the images to perceive. That is, it is necessary to determine which attributes are needed to provide useful groupings of images; which attributes provide information that is useful once the images are found; and which attributes may, or even should, be left to the searcher or researcher to identify. (583, 587)

However, practices vary considerably, depending on the repository, the resources available, the size and requirements of the collection, and perceived user needs. Ultimately, the needs of each particular institution must be independently addressed in determining the depth of description required for its holdings.

Metadata

Metadata is structured data about data, information that facilitates the management and use of other information. The function of metadata is to provide users with a standardized means for intellectual access to holdings. Metadata standards for digital information "can assist by facilitating the transfer of information between hardware and software platforms as technologies evolve.... Resources which are encoded using open standards have a greater chance of remaining accessible after an extended period than resources encoded with proprietary standards" (Preserving Access to Digital Information 2001). However, "it is not enough to use some metadata standard. A metadata standard appropriate to the materials in hand and the intended end-users must be selected" (Baca 2003, 54).

Metadata can identify the name of the work, who created it, who reformatted it, and other descriptive information. It can also provide unique identification of and links to organizations, files, or databases that have more extensive descriptive metadata about the image. Deegan and Tanner (2002) state that metadata is a critical component:

of digital resource development and use, and is needed at all stages in the creation and management of the resource. Any creator of digital objects should take as much care in the creation of the metadata as they do in the creation of the data itself—time and

> effort expended at the creation stage recording quality metadata is likely to save users much grief, and to result in a well-formed digital object that will survive for the long term. Well-formed metadata is the most efficient and effective tool for managing and finding objects in the complex information spaces with which libraries are now dealing. (114)

Unfortunately, no system has yet been widely adopted for tracking the digitization activities of libraries, archives, and museums. The prudent course for information professionals is to understand the current challenges, emerging principles, and best practices before implementing any particular metadata solution. Baca (2003) notes:

> Choosing the most appropriate metadata standard or standards for describing particular collections or materials is only the first step in building an effective, usable information resource. Unless the metadata elements or data structure are populated with the appropriate data values (terminology), the resource will be ineffectual and users will not be able to find what they are looking for, even if it is actually there. Again, there is no one-stop-shopping for the appropriate vocabulary tool for any given project. Rather, builders of information resources should select from the menu of vocabularies most appropriate for describing the providing access points to their particular collections. (52)

There are four types of metadata: administrative, descriptive, preservation, and technical.

Administrative metadata captures the context necessary to understand information resources. It documents:

> the life cycle of [a] ... resource, including data about ordering, acquisition, maintenance, licensing, rights, ownership and provenance. It is essential that the provenance (custodial history) of a digital image object is recorded from, where possible, the time of its creation through all successive changes in custody of ownership. Users and curators must be provided with a sound basis for confidence that a digital image is exactly what it is purported to be.... There should be a clear audit trail of all changes (Anderson et al. 2006, 74).

Box 5.2   Best practices for creating metadata

- When determining which metadata schema to use, take into account the needs and search preferences of users and collaborators.

- Use existing institutional indexes and finding aids as a basis for metadata.

- Metadata creation by professional staff may take less time and require less quality control than training others, even for a small project.

- Base the metadata schema on the existing published schema closest to the institution's needs. The schema can be adapted by adding or omitting elements.

- Use the same name and definition of each element as in the published schema, so as to avoid confusion.

- A set of compatible cataloging rules should accompany the schema. For example, if the schema includes elements drawn from VRA Core (see Box 5.3), the corresponding rules from CCO (see Box 5.4) should be followed.

- Granularity is important. Subdivide elements into the smallest sub-elements needed. Elements can always be merged later.

- Set up editorial and quality control procedures to ensure that the catalog entries conform to the rules.

- Test the schema and the rules thoroughly before it is too late to change them. Discover if the metadata displays correctly on the institution's website and if users are satisfied with the catalog entries.

- Plan where to store the metadata: embedded within the image file, in a separate metadata database, or both.

- Be prepared for change as time passes, and design systems accordingly. For example, more metadata elements or controlled vocabularies may need to be added as the collection expands.

Descriptive metadata attempts to capture the intellectual attributes of the information resource, enabling users to locate, distinguish, and select suitable images on the basis of their subjects.

Preservation metadata is the information about an information resource used to protect it from deterioration or destruction.

Technical metadata assures that the information content of a digital file can be resurrected even if traditional viewing applications associated with that file are no longer available.

Metadata can be embedded in digital images or stored separately. Embedding metadata within the image it describes ensures that the metadata will not be lost, obviates problems of linking between data and metadata, and helps to ensure that the metadata and image will be updated together. Storing metadata separately can simplify the management of the metadata itself and facilitate search and retrieval. Metadata is commonly stored in a database system and linked to the images it describes.

Creating and recording metadata is one of the major costs of image digitization. Although pictorial images can be digitized without cataloging, a digital image collection cannot be created and delivered without metadata. Providing sufficient metadata in a timely, efficient manner for an abundance of digital resources can create a bottleneck in a digital project's workflow. Terras (2008) notes:

> Creating and maintaining metadata about objects[,] and in particular digital information objects, is obviously time-consuming and costly, and a tension exists between the two metadata functions of discovery aid and resource description: metadata creators have to provide enough information to be useful, but cannot afford to be exhaustive. (166)

Sutton (2008) seconds this:

> The biggest challenge [is] balancing the ideal scenario of comprehensive description with the more practical scenario of "good enough" description. The major factors influencing this equation were the limited resources available for digitization in terms of staff, time, and funding. (29)

Puglia (1999) notes that cataloging and indexing can account for nearly a third of the overall cost of a project. Arms (1996) estimates that it would take the cataloging staff of the University of Berkeley libraries 400 years to catalog their collection of 3.5 million images. Lagoze and Payette (2000) add that these costs present:

> considerable challenges to the economics of traditional library cataloging, which creates metadata records characterized by great precision, detail, and professional intervention. Some estimates figure each original library catalog record at $50–70. This high price is impractical in the context of the growth of networked resources and less expensive alternatives are needed for many of these resources. (85)

Metadata creation requires both organizational and subject expertise in order to describe images effectively. Organizational expertise refers to the ability to apply the correct structure, syntax, and use of metadata elements, while subject expertise refers to the ability to generate meaningful descriptions of the images for users. High-quality metadata utilizing both types of expertise is integral to the effective searching, retrieval, use, and preservation of digital resources.

Metadata crosswalks

Using metadata to describe images allows them to be understood by both humans and machines in ways that promote interoperability. Interoperability is the ability of multiple systems with different hardware and software platforms; levels of granularity; controlled vocabularies; data types; and interfaces to exchange data with minimal loss of content and functionality. Using defined metadata schemas and shared transfer protocols, images can be searched for more seamlessly across the network.

Metadata crosswalks—mappings of the elements, semantics, and syntax from one metadata schema to another—further facilitate the exchange of metadata. The degree to which the crosswalk is successful at the item level depends on the similarity of the schemas, the granularity of the elements in the target schema compared to that of the source, and the compatibility of the content rules used to fill the elements of each schema.

Crosswalks are important for collections where resources are drawn from different holding institutions and are expected to act as a whole, perhaps with a single search engine applied. While crosswalks are key, they are also labor intensive to develop and maintain. The mapping of schemas with fewer elements, or less granularity, to those with more elements, or more granularity, is problematic. These problems have led to significant frustration for users who want consistent metadata inter-operability across digital imaging products and services. Manufac-turers of digital imaging hardware, software, and services spend substan-tial resources dealing with these problems. Until these complexities are resolved, the problems will continue to cost users and industry both time and resources.

Image description practices

Schellenberg (1965) devotes the final chapter of *Management of Archives* to the arrangement and description of visual materials. He notes, "The methods of arranging and describing pictorial records have not been fully defined, much less standardized" (322). Since the publication of his seminal book, formal standards such as *Describing Archives: A content standard (DACS)*, *Graphic Materials*, and *Rules for Archival Description (RAD)*, have been developed for the description of visual materials. For example, *ISAD(G): General international standard archival description* defines multilevel principles, such as moving from the broad to the specific, linking hierarchical levels, and basic descriptive elements. These elements include creator names, titles, dates, administrative history, scope and content, and locations of originals and copies (International Council on Archives 2000). Baca (2003) comments:

> Increasingly, institutions and projects, especially collaborative initiatives in a particular subject area, are finding that the most effective thing they can do to serve their internal and external users is to build their own thesauri and classification systems, using terms from established, broadly accepted subject vocabu-laries like Library of Congress Subject Headings, or the Art & Architecture Thesaurus, but also adding both preferred and variant terms from the specific field of study and from sources both printed and human, both expert and non-expert. Some leading museum collection management systems include built-in subject vocabularies and thesaurus building tools to facilitate this process. (52)

While descriptive standards provide for consistency, repositories employ descriptive systems suited to their own holdings, not to universal access, and description continues to be idiosyncratic (Pugh 2005). Zinkham (1986) states:

> A single list of standard terms from which catalogers and researchers can choose indexing and retrieval vocabulary is needed ... because of the great variety of media and pictorial types and because of the broad range of users of graphic materials, whose knowledge and experience vary. While an extensive and often informational vocabulary is employed in the descriptive portion of the catalog record, indexing terms should be controlled. Reconciling variant terms by designating a preferred indexing term not only simplifies the cataloger's task but also makes retrieval most efficient. For example, the standard term "dry plate photo-negatives" lessens confusion about "silver gelatine glass negatives," "glass plates," and "dry plates." (v)

With the advent of computers, some institutions used MARC records to provide subject indexing for large pictorial collections through individual collection-level records (Ritzenthaler and Vogt-O'Connor 2006). The MARC records pointed users to a finding aid for a particular collection for more detailed information. Since the finding aids were generally paper based, and often available only locally at the institution, users would have to view them in person.

Item-level MARC cataloging of images, while in some cases desirable, was often neither warranted nor economically feasible (Ritzenthaler and Vogt-O'Connor 2006). The hierarchical format and electronic access capabilities of the Encoded Archival Description (EAD) finding aid, however, offer the possibility of a more powerful, flexible alternative. EAD was developed as a way of marking the data contained in paper-based finding aids so that they can be searched and displayed online. EAD promised a more sophisticated way not only to produce searchable text but to eventually provide descriptions in an environment that would facilitate sophisticated cross-collection searching (Pitti 1999). EAD indexes image collections by providing access points at the collection or item level, depending on the needs of the institution, collection, and users. As EADs evolve, their content-specific indexing capabilities will make them a powerful resource for standardized access to visual collections.

The Dublin Core Metadata Element Set arose from discussions at a 1995 workshop sponsored by Online Computer Library Center (OCLC) and the National Center for Supercomputing Applications (NCSA). As the workshop was held in Dublin, Ohio, the element set was named the Dublin Core. The continuing development of the Dublin Core and related specifications is managed by the Dublin Core Metadata Initiative (DCMI).

Dublin Core is designed to be easy to use and less expensive to implement than more complex metadata schemes. The core set of fifteen data elements can be used to describe and to facilitate discovery of images, capturing information regarding the title, identifier, creator, contributor, publisher, language, description, subject, coverage, date, type, relation, format, source, and rights of a digital image. None of the elements is mandatory and all can be repeated and expanded if needed. While the Dublin Core metadata schema serves as a functional framework for exposing metadata, the standard is open to interpretation. Use of the elements may vary among institutions. Its simple nature is not suited to capturing descriptions with a high level of granularity, but it focuses on interoperability and international consensus. Terras (2008) states that Dublin Core:

> is not designed in particular to capture comprehensive descriptions of graphical metadata, but can be easily extended in that direction. The most widely used and supported metadata set in the library community, the Dublin Core provides a lowest common denominator in mapping and describing diverse information resources, and has become the most readily appropriated metadata standard for describing online digital resources. (172)

Dublin Core is especially attractive to cultural heritage institutions because of the number of commercial systems that have adopted and supported it, including CONTENTdm and Greenstone, two off-the-shelf digital asset management systems. Dublin Core is also compliant with the Open Archives Initiative Protocol for Metadata Harvesting (OAI-PMH), which allows for repository interoperability by allowing institutions to export their records in Dublin Core for inclusion in search services based on metadata systems of varying types.

Current practices for structuring image collections include lists, indexes, directories, catalogs, thesauri, taxonomies, ontologies, typologies, metadata, templates, or topic maps. Retrieval systems and digital asset management (DAM) software are based on language, particularly

Table 5.1 Dublin Core metadata elements and their definitions

Element name	Definition
Contributor	Person(s) or organization(s) in addition to those specified in the Creator element who have made significant intellectual contributions to the image, but on a secondary basis.
Coverage	The spatial locations and temporal duration characteristics of the resource.
Creator	The person(s) or organization(s) primarily responsible for making the image.
Date	A period of time associated with an event in the life cycle of the image.
Description	The content description of the image.
Format	The file format, physical medium, or dimensions of the image.
Identifier	A unique reference to the image within a given context.
Language	A language of the image.
Publisher	An entity responsible for making the image available.
Relation	The relationship to other images.
Rights	Information about rights to the image.
Source	A related reference from which the image is derived.
Subject	The topic of the image, which includes keywords, phrases, or classification descriptors that describe the image's content.
Title	A name given to the image by the Creator or Publisher.
Type	The nature or genre of the image.

Source: Dublin Core Metadata Initiative Metadata Terms:
    http://dublincore.org/documents/dcmi-terms/#elements.

keywords, because words are extractable from documents. For images, there is no language to extract, only language to apply. Keywords provide content-based access points to images because they label the objects being photographed. To a lesser extent, they can also be concept based, detailing an image's features, attributes, and characteristics.

Goodrum (2005) writes, "Surrogates such as keywords, titles, captions, or cataloging records function not only as attributes against which a query may be matched, but also provide support for browsing, navigation, relevance, judgments, and query formation" (46). However, detailed, consistent description still has limited usage because "picture searching often involves more browsing and less construction of complex queries" (Pisciotta 2003, 130).

Box 5.3 Data structure standards

CDWA and CDWA Lite (Categories for the Description of Works of Art)

www.getty.edu/research/conducting_research/standards/cdwa/index.html
These rules "describe the content of art databases by articulating a conceptual framework for describing and accessing information about works of art, architecture, other material culture, groups and collections of works, and related images."

DC (Dublin Core Metadata Element Set)

http://dublincore.org/documents/dces/
DC is "a vocabulary of fifteen properties for use in resource description. The name 'Dublin' is due to its origin at a 1995 invitational workshop in Dublin, Ohio; 'core' because its elements are broad and generic, usable for describing a wide range of resources."

EAC-CPF (Encoded Archival Context–Corporate Bodies, Persons, and Families)

http://eac.staatsbibliothek-berlin.de/
EAC-CPF "primarily addresses the description of individuals, families and corporate bodies that create, preserve, use and are responsible for and/or associated with records in a variety of ways."

EAD (Encoded Archival Description)

www.loc.gov/ead
EAD was developed to "investigate the desirability and feasibility of developing a nonproprietary encoding standard for machine-readable finding aids such as inventories, registers, indexes, and other documents created by archives, libraries, museums, and manuscript repositories to support the use of their holdings."

IPTC Photo Metadata Standard (International Press Telecommunications Council)

www.iptc.org/std/photometadata/specification/IPTC-PhotoMetadata(200907)_1.pdf

Box 5.3   Data structure standards (*Cont'd*)

"IPTC Photo Metadata provides data about photographs and the values can be processed by software."

MADS (Metadata Authority Description Schema)

www.loc.gov/standards/mads

"MADS is a MARC21-compatible XML format for the type of data carried in records in the MARC Authorities format.... Consistency with MODS [see below] was a goal as much as possible."

MARC21 (Machine-Readable Cataloging)

www.loc.gov/marc/

"MARC formats are standards for the representation and communication of bibliographic and related information in machine-readable form."

METS (Metadata Encoding & Transmission Standard)

www.loc.gov/standards/mets/

METS is a "standard for encoding descriptive, administrative, and structural metadata regarding objects within a digital library."

MODS (Metadata Object Description Schema)

www.loc.gov/standards/mods/

MODS is a "schema for a bibliographic element set that may be used for a variety of purposes, and particularly for library applications."

VRA Core 4.0

www.vraweb.org/projects/vracore4/

VRA Core 4.0 is a "data standard for the cultural heritage community that was developed by the Visual Resources Association's Data Standards Committee. It consists of a metadata element set (units of information such as title, location, date, etc.), as well as an initial blueprint for how those elements can be hierarchically structured. The element set provides a categorical organization for the description of works of visual culture as well as the images that document them."

Box 5.4 Data content standards

AACR2 (Anglo-American Cataloguing Rules, Second Edition)

www.aacr2.org/

These rules are "designed for use in the construction of catalogues and other lists in general libraries of all sizes. The rules cover the description of, and the provision of access points for, all library materials commonly collected at the present time."

CCO (Cataloging Cultural Objects)

www.vrafoundation.org/ccoweb/

"CCO covers many types of cultural objects, including architecture, archaeological sites and artifacts, and some functional objects from the realm of material culture, but its primary emphasis is on art, including but not limited to paintings, sculptures, prints, manuscripts, photographs, and other visual media."

DACS (Describing Archives: A Content Standard)

www.archivists.org/governance/standards/dacs.asp

These rules are used "to create any type or level of description of archival and manuscript materials including catalog records and finding aids."

Graphic Materials

www.loc.gov/rr/print/gm/graphmat.html

"For groups of pictures as well as individual items, the guidelines cover transcribing and devising titles; stating creators, producers, and dates; expressing quantities, media, and dimensions; and writing subject, user advisory, and other kinds of notes."

ISAAR (CPF) (International Standard Archival Authority Record for Corporate Bodies, Persons, and Families)

www.icacds.org.uk/eng/ISAAR(CPF)2ed.pdf

"This standard provides guidance for preparing archival authority records which provide descriptions of entities (corporate bodies,

Box 5.4 Data content standards (*Cont'd*)

---

persons and families) associated with the creation and maintenance of archives."

ISAD(G) (International Standard Archival Description)

www.ica.org/en/node/30000

"This standard provides general guidance for the preparation of archival descriptions. It is to be used in conjunction with existing national standards or as the basis for the development of national standards."

RAD (Rules for Archival Description)

www.cdncouncilarchives.ca/archdesrules.html

"These rules aim to provide a consistent and common foundation for the description of archival material based on traditional archival principles. The rules can be applied to the description of archival fonds, series, collections, and discrete items."

Box 5.5 Data value standards

AAT (Art & Architecture Thesaurus Online)

www.getty.edu/research/conducting_research/vocabularies/aat/
AAT is a "structured vocabulary of around 34,000 concepts, including 131,000 terms, descriptions, bibliographic citations, and other information relating to fine art, architecture, decorative arts, archival materials, and material culture."

LCSH (Library of Congress Authorities—Subject Headings)

http://authorities.loc.gov/
LSCH is comprised of a thesaurus of subject headings maintained by the United States Library of Congress, for use in bibliographic records.

(*Cont'd*)

Box 5.5   Data value standards (*Cont'd*)

TGM (Thesaurus of Graphic Materials)

www.loc.gov/rr/print/tgm1/

TGM "provides a substantial body of terms for subject indexing of pictorial materials, particularly the large general collections of historical images which are found in many libraries, historical societies, archives, and museums."

TGN (Thesaurus of Geographic Names)

www.getty.edu/research/conducting_research/vocabularies/tgn/

TGN "contains around 895,000 records, including around 1,115,000 names, place types, coordinates, and descriptive notes."

ULAN (Union List of Artist Names)

www.getty.edu/research/conducting_research/vocabularies/ulan/

ULAN is "a structured vocabulary containing around 127,000 records, including 375,000 names and biographical and bibliographic information about artists and architects, including a wealth of variant names, pseudonyms, and language variants."

Rather than designing more effective language-based algorithms, retrieval system designers should reinterpret keyword searches based on information-seeking behavior, cognition, and memory. Newer approaches like tagging and algorithmic or heuristic browsing provide more search versatility. Browsing based on both content and concept remains on the edge of discovery.

Online collections offer structuring ingenuity because digital images can more easily belong to multiple categories simultaneously, whereas analog images cannot. Collections have evolved from analog images arranged in mutually exclusive categories, to digital images tagged with any number of labels, allowing users to focus on the interrelationships between the images. With online collections, folksonomy, or social tagging, allows viewers to apply semantic keywords to images, which could cultivate deeper semantic associations between the multiple meanings of the images.

Description for digitization initiatives

Thorough, informative description is a key to improving the representation of historical images. The better the cataloging, the richer the contextualizing information that surrounds the photographs and the better able users are to appreciate them in their historical context. Digital images require sufficient descriptive data to render them available, understandable, and usable for as long as they have continuing value. The types of information needed to describe digital images will differ from, and may exceed, those needed to describe analog images, but the basic purpose of description remains the same.

For digital conversion projects, it is usually assumed that indexing has already been completed to an adequate level before the digitization begins, but this is rarely the case. Description is often either begun from scratch or improved on as part of the project. Much of the data required for image records appears as annotations on the original images. Therefore, no matter what the form of the access records, information is usually assembled from various sources. Since description is not the main outcome of a project, it is often done in a perfunctory way. Access records for digital surrogates involve far more than simple digital conversion of the existing finding aid.

Layne (1994) suggests, "Rather than devoting time to extraordinarily detailed or complicated indexing, or to elaborate parsing schemes that refine verbal searches, it might be better to concentrate on indexing the basic elements of an image and rely on scanning … to make the fine distinctions" (586). Keister (1994) states:

> Presentation of an image surrogate … addresses the aesthetic or emotional need of the user—a highly subjective need not appropriate for the cataloguer to consider. Any picture reference librarian knows that patrons ask for "dramatic pictures," "grabbers," etc.… Watching patrons searching images … shows that a most interesting dynamic occurs in which words, in carefully constructed catalog records, introduce the user to selections of images; and the user then reviews, analyzes, and verifies with words again before finally arriving at the selection. The user constantly checks … to see which image "works," that is, communicates most effectively the desired message. (17)

Image collections with thumbnail presentation of images and metadata provide the possibility of such access. Cawkell (1993) states that systems like this "immediately bring to bear the most efficient selective system by far—the human eye/brain" (411). Hedstrom (2000) states, "The electronic era holds out the promise of richer, more detailed descriptive systems that are incorporated into the design of automated applications and implemented as records are created" (393).

Metadata for information management

As with other aspects of digital imaging, decisions about investing in metadata will be guided by a digitization initiative's overall purpose and audience. Accordingly, information professionals must evaluate the costs and benefits of creating and maintaining different kinds of metadata at different levels of granularity. Information professionals:

> should take a lead in researching and developing new forms of access, and finding opportunities to apply them to special collections.... Adequate online metadata is an essential condition for good quality access to both the original and digitized versions of materials. Minimal description is better than none.... Special collections description is increasingly open to interaction with the community of users. Archivists and librarians should encourage and take advantage of these interactions in order to promote access.... New definitions need to be created for determining the scope of digital special collections, so that stakeholders can understand the nature of special collections professionals' responsibilities. (ARL 2009)

It is useful to consider the ways in which users will approach images in the collection and the different aspects of the images. Having a clear understanding of the images and the ways users view them will enable a more critical evaluation of potential metadata schemas and vocabularies and a better assemblage of a metadata framework that works for users and catalogers.

An effective method of selecting and using metadata is to create a set of elements that will best describe the images. When complete, the elements should be assessed against available standard metadata and vocabularies, and the approaches to metadata handling utilized by other institutions with similar aims and objectives should be investigated. This approach ensures that images will be described in ways that make them accessible for their intended purposes, saves time in developing cataloging rules and accepted field terms and mappings, and ensures a greater likelihood that the images will be interoperable with other related collections.

Due to the nature of photographs, a standardized approach for description is ideal, but compromises must be made. Not all images can be indexed completely, nor can all resources be expended on indexing only a few collections. Approaches should be equitable, reasonable, and within the means of the institution. While challenges will be encountered when working with visual materials, images hold a wealth of information that justifies the additional effort needed to make them accessible.

6

Digitization

Abstract: Cultural heritage institutions play an important role in preserving and providing access to cultural heritage materials, and digitizing these collections has become an essential task in fulfilling this function. Information professionals must engage the tools and practices of digitization in order to capture, preserve, and disseminate visual culture for posterity. This chapter analyzes the issues information professionals should be familiar with so they can form effective strategies to design, fund, and manage digitization projects. Decisions on in-house or outsourced digitization, costs, staffing, collaboration, benchmarking, quality assessment, and content management systems must be determined, based on what is most cost-effective and beneficial for the host institution. With this in mind, this chapter explores the fundamentals of a digitization project, focusing on practical considerations and presenting an overview of the managerial, technical, and financial issues associated with digitizing cultural heritage materials.

Keywords: benchmarking, collaboration, digitization, postproduction, project planning, quality assessment

It's not about moving pixels, it's about pictures that move us. (John Weiss)

Digital imaging combined with computer storage and retrieval expands and restructures ... memory and allows it to function in new ways. It electronically accelerates the mechanisms of the visual record, enables the weaving of complex networks of interconnection between images to establish multiple and perhaps incommensurable layers of meaning, allows heterarchical association and access patterns to develop, and transforms the museum without walls into the even less spatialized virtual museum. Mnemosyne has become a digital matrix. (William J. Mitchell, 2001)

The definition of a medium, particularly photography, is not autonomous or self-governing, but heteronymous, dependent on other media. It derives less from what it is *technologically* than what it is *culturally*. Photography is what we do with it. And what we do with it depends on what we do with other image technologies. (David Campany, 2003)

Introduction

Digitization initiatives require a tremendous amount of strategic planning before a single item can be successfully digitized. A digital project is not a linear process in which one task follows another, but a complex system of interrelated tasks in which each decision influences the next. Deegan and Tanner (2002) write, "Digital capture is only one aspect of the many processes involved in the highly complex chain of activities that are attendant upon the creation, management, use and preservation of digital objects for the long term." Digitization, as defined in this book, is a process that includes the selection, assessment, and prioritization of images; project management and tracking; preparation of originals for digitization; metadata collection and creation; digitizing; quality control; data collection and management; submission of images to the database; and evaluation of the outcome.

Digitization requires close management because of the rates of change inherent in digital projects, the complex nature of digitization processes, and the level of staff training required. Lynch (2002) notes that cultural heritage institutions:

> have a wealth of experience and a large number of successful projects (not to mention some highly educational failures) to build upon. With the exception of relatively esoteric materials in specialized formats or that have some really unusual characteristics ... the research questions are less about how to do it at all and more about how to optimize—how to [digitize] more efficiently or effectively, how to be sure that you've chosen the most appropriate strategies and technologies.

In essence, best practices, or accepted methodologies for completing tasks effectively, are needed. Hughes (2004) notes:

> In relation to the digitisation of cultural and heritage materials, best practices, like their analogue antecedents, are simply working practices and procedures that can provide a safety net for practitioners as they navigate all aspects of the digitisation workflow. Following these markers will give a reasonable expectation of success and add value to projects in terms of their long-term consistency. (199)

By employing best practices in the way digital images are created, managed, and preserved, information professionals will ensure the relevance of the images to future generations and justify the investments made in digitization projects.

Since interest in digital media began, a great deal has been learned about the best ways to plan, implement, and manage digital projects, and pioneering projects have resulted in the evolution of recommended procedures. In the beginning, the methodologies for the production and management of digital projects were extemporized. With new, evolving technologies, and prior to the widespread use of networking capabilities, incompatible resources with short life spans were created. However, technology has now advanced sufficiently that cultural heritage institutions are able apply standards forged by seasoned international communities. Applying these guidelines to digital projects greatly enhances the widespread use and viability of projects, and maximizes both the investment made in them and the potential that technology can offer to scholarly endeavors.

The many parties involved in standardizing the digitization of cultural heritage materials emphasize the extreme difficulty of the process. While the individuality of each institution will be reflected in its customized digitization methods, the similarities between institutions should be emphasized because they have created a wealth of shared experiences that will save time and money for organizations embarking on the digitization process. With this in mind, this chapter explores the fundamentals of a digitization project, focusing on practical considerations.

Project objectives

Information professionals take their responsibilities seriously as stewards of the collections entrusted to their care, ensuring that assets remain safe and accessible to users. The demand for increased online access to collections, coupled with limited fiscal and staff resources, makes balancing the two a continuing challenge. Creating explicit objectives at the conception of a digitization project will assure that the project is successful and sustainable. Staffing and fiscal resources need to be evaluated before the project is undertaken, and the aims of the project should be realistic when compared to the resources available.

Digital projects should also be reviewed for their continuing applicability. Just as some materials may be unsuitable for digitizing, the value of existing projects may be reconsidered from time to time. In some cases, additional resources may be expended when enhanced accessibility will benefit users. Conversely, some digital projects may outlive their value and should be discontinued.

While planning a project, information professionals must understand the institution's mission and where the digital project fits into its goals, and assess existing resources against those that need to be acquired. They also need to establish standards that will be adhered to while conducting the digitization project; to begin the documentation process so as to assure that decisions are well communicated; to plan the implementation of the project; and to evaluate the project and provide direction.

The scope of the project and the characteristics of the photographs will translate into image-capture specifications and procedures for building digital collections. Evaluating the characteristics of the images to be digitized is part of the planning process, which involves determining the number of images to be digitized, identifying source formats, considering the images' sizes, assessing unusual characteristics, and reviewing the condition of originals. The project should be planned to progress efficiently, and the workflow should be well organized. Digital equipment must be chosen to optimize the quality and level of production, the appropriate hardware and software must be selected, and image capture and editing rules must be set so as to maximize efficiency.

Box 6.1   **Best practices for planning a digitization project**

- Take as much time as needed at the outset of a project to define goals and outcomes.

- Insist on the highest quality of technical work that the institution can afford.

- Factor in costs and capabilities for long-term maintenance of the digitized images.

- Cultivate a high level of staff involvement.

- Write a project plan, budget, timeline, and other planning documents.

- Budget time for training.

- Plan a workflow based upon the results of scanning and cataloging a representative sample of material.

The success of digital projects hinges not on technology, but on project planning. Since digitization is a relatively new endeavor, institutions may too often concentrate on technology before deciding on a project's purpose. However, technology should never drive digital projects; instead, user-based desiderata should be determined first, and only then should the appropriate technology be selected to meet a project's objectives.

Kenney and Chapman (1996a) state:

> Digital conversion efforts will be economically viable only if they focus on selecting and creating electronic resources for long-term use.... Retrospective sources should be selected carefully based on their intellectual content; that digital surrogates should effectively capture that intellectual content; and that access should be offered to those surrogates in a more timely, usable, or cost-effective manner than is possible with the original source documents. In essence, we believe that long-term utility should be defined *by the informational value and functionality* of digital images, not limited by technical decisions made at the point of conversion or anywhere else along the digitization chain.

Information professionals should develop projects that can be utilized by a variety of user groups for comprehensive research, learning, and general informational purposes. To this end, they should establish criteria outlining collection selection, metadata creation, and systems for access that address the varied interests and needs of users. Digital collections should also enhance users' understanding of the value of the images, their authenticity, archival context, and historical significance. Institutions should provide a stable, scalable, and sustainable platform for the delivery and management of digital content, as well as strive to deliver content in ever-evolving ways—challenging information professionals to create a premier research experience for users.

Cost estimates

Digitization projects are labor intensive, require extensive expertise, are organizationally and logistically complex, and demand an enduring commitment to continued maintenance, migration, and updating. They are a unique and often unprecedented expense, usually in response to a new funding opportunity, and should not be compared to—or substituted

Box 6.2 Best practices for digitization

- Scan at the highest resolution appropriate to the informational content of the originals.

- Scan once. Scanning at an appropriate level of quality avoids the need for future rescanning and rehandling of originals.

- Create and store master image files, which can be used to produce derivative files for a variety of current and future user needs.

- Use system components that are non-proprietary.

- Use image file formats and compression techniques that conform to industry standards.

- Use system-independent and widely used and supported file formats.

for—existing expenses and activities. Virtually every step in digitization involves human intervention and skill, and these costs are unlikely to decrease.

Projects have to take into account start-up and infrastructural costs as well as the costs for running the project. Costs may include selection, preparation, and conservation of original source materials; metadata creation; digital capture costs, including the purchase of hardware, software and peripheral equipment; quality control of images and metadata; the maintenance of the technical infrastructure, including hardware maintenance and network costs; ongoing maintenance of images and metadata, including perdurable storage costs; rights clearance; staff costs, including technical support, project management, web programming and interface design staff, and training; user evaluation; and documentation. Kenney and Chapman (1996a) add:

> In an ideal world, we would be able to create digital masters from hard copy sources without regard to cost, and to produce multiple derivatives tailored to the individual user upon request. In the real world, of course, costs must be taken into account when selecting, converting, and making accessible digital collections. Those looking for immediate cost recovery in choosing digital over hard copy or analog conversion will be disappointed to learn that preliminary

findings indicate that these costs can be staggering. Outside funding may be available to initiate such efforts, but the investments for continuing systematic conversion of collections to develop a critical mass of retrospective digitized material, electronic access requirements, and long-term maintenance of digital libraries will fall to institutions both individually and collectively. These costs will be sustainable only if the benefits accrued are measurable, considerable, and sustainable.

The greatest expense is cataloging the images, followed by a succession of labor-intensive procedures such as locating, reviewing, and assembling source images; preparing and tracking them; and controlling their quality. Technology has a short life cycle, which means the expenditure of replacing systems after an average of three years, as well as the significant investment required for staff to learn the latest systems and applications. More difficult to quantify are the project's disruption of personnel, facilities, and circulation of photographs over extended periods. Given these demands, few organizations will rescan their holdings more than once, so collections should be digitized correctly the first time.

Hazen et al. (1998) state: "Cost-benefit analysis assesses the relationship between functionality, demand, and expense. Limited resources and competing demands on organizational time and energy mean that the analysis must be rigorous and complete." Available figures for expenditures related to digitizing projects are often misleading. Although the prices of computer storage and processing power continue to fall, most budget projections simply extrapolate from available information about current price structures. Analyses also often fail to account for certain efforts that, were they included, would alter calculations significantly; functions such as preparation of images for scanning, indexing, metadata creation, post-scanning processing, and unavoidable file management may not be factored into cost estimations.

Plans to digitize collections must consider the changes this type of endeavor will bring to the workplace and how a new set of tasks will affect the organization. Institutions should acknowledge at the outset the continuing benefits of temporary cost increases for training and equipment. While equipment costs often draw the greatest attention, support expenses are usually larger and have more comprehensive implications for the institution. The rapid turnover in technology requires frequent migration and upgrades. If an institution is to transition successfully to a digital environment, it must learn from the outset how to allocate resources interminability.

Digitization requires a long-standing institutional commitment to traditional preservation, integration of technology into information management procedures, and leadership in developing appropriate definitions and standards for digital preservation. The risk of loss is high, far higher than in most other programs and activities carried out in a cultural institution. Lynch (2002) observes:

> Every digitization project that I know of, every funder of digitization projects that I know of, is acutely sensitive to this issue of sustainability, of trying to avoid the dilemma where we fund the creation of materials that we cannot economically sustain in the long run.

Sustainability is often pushed aside by more immediate concerns. Regardless of the quality and robustness of the digital resources created by a digitization project, they will not last long if the project cannot fund their maintenance.

Developing prototype projects and feasibility studies based on real costs is important because the experience of working with one's own collections is one of the best ways to forecast project costs. In many cases, a few items are sufficient. A technical pilot may also be considered so as to ensure that any problems with the technical workflow are resolved before the project commences.

In-house or outsourced digitization

Digitization can either be performed in-house or outsourced. Digitizing in-house implies that a department of the institution captures the images, supplying hardware and software, trained personnel, and overhead. Outsourcing means entering into a contract with a vendor who will receive the images, convert them, and return the originals and the required digital files. Both in-house and outsourced options should be considered when embarking on a digitization project. Whether to digitize in-house or via outsourcing will depend on the scope, nature, fragility, and uniqueness of the materials, the project budget, and institutional resources.

Given the high cost of scanning and related equipment, outsourcing is advantageous because vendors bring their experience of working on many similar projects. Few institutions have sufficient budget to keep pace with the latest hardware and software. Vendors maintain the latest

---

Box 6.3 Advantages of in-house and outsourced digitization

In-house

- Development of digital imaging project experience.

- Control over imaging process, quality control, and handling of originals.

- Requirements for image quality can be adjusted as needed, not clearly defined at the outset of the pilot project.

- Direct participation in development of image collections that best suits users.

Outsourced

- Higher productivity level and economies of scale.

- Expertise of digital image specialists.

- Payment is for the cost of scanning services only, not equipment.

- Responsible for technology failure and correction of errors.

- Vendor has premises devoted to scanning, suited to electrical and technical requirements.

---

equipment, employ specialists, and are knowledgeable about their services and costs.

However, outsourcing imaging rather than developing in-house digitization services is not always the best solution. Information professionals may be motivated to invest in the space, staff, training, and equipment needed for digitization if they already administer or have access to a scanning studio within the broader organization. Additionally, the institution may decide to invest in developing expertise that can be leveraged for other services. While using vendors is convenient, the experience that would have been gained during the execution of the outsourced work will be lost to the institution at the end of the project; performing digitization in-house results in the acquisition of this specialized knowledge. In-house imaging also allows for small-scale experimentation without having to write technical specifications and contracts. A pilot project may serve as a prelude to contracting out the bulk of the work and is often a necessary step in the learning process.

Box 6.4 Best practices for selecting a vendor

- Develop an initial concept of the project and its goals.

- Identify potential vendors.

- Send a request for information (RFI) to explain the goals of the project.

- Establish a project methodology and quality requirements.

- Develop a short list of vendors.

- Write a request for proposal (RFP) and send it to the short list, along with samples of the material to be scanned.

- Communicate with the vendors while they work on their responses, including making site visits and meeting with them when possible.

- Evaluate and compare the vendors' proposals, select the best, and sign the contract.

Working in-house is suitable when a project is small or can be broken down into segments; if the institution has skilled staff or staff with the incentive to learn and has support from the administration for in-depth training; and if the institution already has appropriate equipment or the funding to acquire it. By developing digital imaging expertise internally, even if this approach results in higher per-item costs for digital surrogates, the organization will be positioning itself to digitize collections into the future.

To work in-house, an appropriate environment and hardware and software system must be in place before digitization can begin. Elements include scanners, digital cameras, copy stands, and other hardware; a computing infrastructure to which the hardware is connected; and software for image capture, processing, metadata, and quality control. The working environment should be appropriate to the material being digitized, paying attention to light, humidity, vibration, and the handling of the originals.

Candidate images will have to be moved to the location of the digitization equipment—either to another building or to another city. Although outsourcing usually entails sending images to vendors outside

Figure 6.1 Digitization workflow comparing in-house and outsourcing options

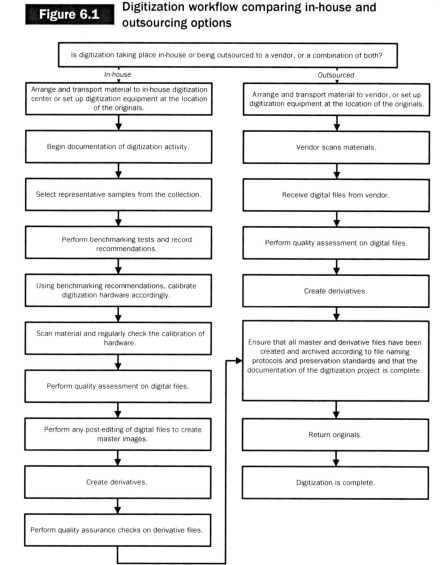

the institution, some vendors may be able to scan on site. This offers some of the benefits of in-house projects, such as closer oversight of the vendor, but providing an appropriate work area, as well as security, insurance, and other details will still be required.

Staffing

Staffing needs for digital projects depend on the size and complexity of the project. Training existing staff and management to work on digitization projects is a key component of change management within the institution. Jones (2001) writes:

> Digital projects require new skills. Project planning should allow time to teach current staff new technologies. Even if an outside vendor completes a project, or new staff is hired specifically to work on a digital project, permanent staff should at least learn the basic theories and practices of digitization. Institutions often hire short-term staff for digitization projects[,] which can result in the loss of digital expertise when the project ends.

The digital age is moving memory institutions into new paradigms of delivering both services and content, and this alteration brings with it a need for training so as to gain knowledge and experience in managing information in a hybrid environment. Similarly, to reflect this shift, a focus on appropriate academic preparation for those entering cultural heritage professions is needed (Marcum 1998).

Unless the staff working on the project have significant experience from prior projects, training is required. Some skills, such as in the use of digitization technology, can be learned while performing digitization tasks, while others, such as handling of source materials, require training in advance. A small core of personnel who are trained and have gained experienced on the project is preferred to a larger group that may change its membership frequently.

Working as a team, the staff for digitization projects include many participants with different areas of expertise. The following list describes some of the positions that a digital project may need, with the understanding that the responsibilities can be reduced or expanded, depending on the nature of the project and the size of the institution.

- A project manager oversees daily operations and maintains the budget, timeline, and workflow.

- A collections assessor selects originals, checks their condition and makes conservation recommendations, rehouses originals as necessary, and reshelves them once digitization and cataloging are complete.

- A database manager creates and maintains databases for the project.

- A scanning technician handles original objects, creates scans and surrogates, and produces backup files on the storage media.

- A quality-control technician checks the image files generated by the scanning technician against benchmarks.

- A cataloger creates or edits records for the digital images of originals included in the project.

- A web manager designs and maintains the website housing the project.

In many institutions, a steering committee for the project functions as an executive board and includes curators, archivists, and subject specialists. An advisory committee provides counsel on the project's focus and direction. Members can include the steering committee, with additional appointments from external organizations bringing areas of expertise to the project. Subcommittees may supply more focused technical, academic, or editorial support. In small projects, the steering committee may consist of only a few members of upper management, and the advisory board may include the group and members of the board of directors.

Collaboration

Collaboration is increasingly a factor in all aspects of work in libraries, archives, and museums and is often a prerequisite for digitization initiatives at local, national, and international levels. Such partnerships have the potential to broaden access to images, ensure their long-term maintenance, create revenue-sharing opportunities, maximize existing resources for digital content, and serve as excellent public relations for both partners.

However, such projects may cause tension between technologists and cultural heritage professionals. In many organizations, physical and cultural barriers exist between archival, library, or curatorial staff and IT professionals, despite the fact that memory organizations are increasingly dependent upon technological infrastructures to support everyday activities.

Learning to work together at the local level provides a valuable platform for making larger partnerships work. ARL (2009) comments:

> A major theme that emerges during digital curation is the need for partnerships and collaborations.... Defining requirements, identifying partners with the capabilities and capacity to meet those requirements, and routine monitoring of their performance need to become an integral part of strategies for managing digital materials in special collections. (28)

Taking advantage of the frameworks that can support cooperation and understanding the benefits of partnerships will build a foundation for successful collaboration. Partnerships should always foster the institutional missions, visions, and values of all parties, and understanding such goals at the outset will avoid problems. Agreements should be steadfast in regard to the provision of access to digital collections over the long term.

Relationships between institutions have many benefits. More experienced practitioners share technical standards and best practices, and collaboration can facilitate technology transfer by developing opportunities for resource building and development in smaller institutions that have limited technology infrastructure or expertise. Additionally, opportunities for staff development are created by partnering with early adopters who can share their skills. Collaborative initiatives may increase opportunities for funding, as many granting agencies and foundations encourage partnership projects, especially those that provide a basis for developing a shared information infrastructure. Integrating collections and resources builds virtual, reunified collections that have the potential to reach larger, disparate audiences and achieve a greater breadth of educational goals. Mutual metadata and delivery mechanisms result in improved resource discovery for users as well. Savings from sharing the costs of conversion by volume may be realized, as larger projects are more cost-effective on a per-image basis.

Box 6.5 **Best practices for collaboration**

- Cooperate with other institutions whenever possible so as to achieve the greatest benefits.

- Define the scope of the project, including appropriate collections and the level of indexing.

- Define the roles and areas of responsibility of the participating institutions.

- Establish measurable objectives to evaluate the success of the project upon completion.

- Agree on long-term maintenance of the digital images and their associated metadata.

- Share experiences and results with other institutions.

Documentation

Documentation, in the context of digitization, may be described as text that provides a thorough conveyance of the thoughts and processes behind the construction of digital collections. The National Information Standards Organization's (NISO) (2007) *A Framework of Guidance for Building Good Digital Collections* states:

> In the non-digital realm, the authenticity of documents is often determined through forensics such as paleography, examination of physical characteristics, and comparison of handwritten signatures. For digital objects, such physical clues do not exist, and the importance of documentation increases proportionately. The user wants to know the origin of the digital object, whether or not the object has been altered since its creation, and if so, how and by whom. (55)

Documentation explains whether the collection was comprehensive, and if not, how material was selected and why. It details any important decisions made in the planning and creation of a project. Technical documentation describes the rationale for the creation of the digital collection and the repository that houses it online, allowing anyone who wishes to reuse the images to understand that rationale. In effect, documentation preserves the institutional memory of a project. Hazen et al. (1998) affirm that:

> Projects based on careful review, analysis, and planning can yield electronic resources that are functional and faithful to the original sources, and that support new kinds of scholarship. A detailed plan of work, regular assessment of progress, closely documented adjustments and corrections, and the retention of other project-related data can strengthen the knowledge base for future efforts. Each success, as well as each failure, will bring us closer to fulfilling the promises of the electronic environment.

Technology changes with time, and thus solutions developed by an earlier project may become outmoded. However, if new projects can consult the documentation produced by others, they may be able to adapt existing resources or discover solutions to similar problems and save significant amounts of time and money. Documentation enables

Figure 6.2 Digitization overview

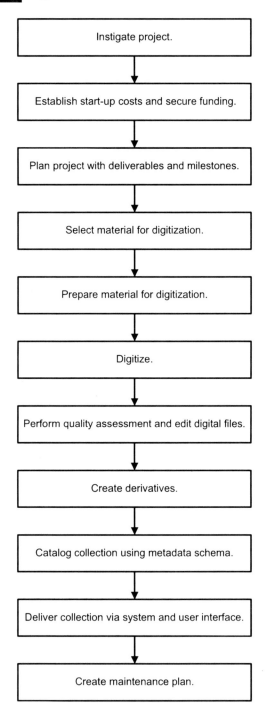

users to access as much information as possible about the contents of the resource and the decisions taken in its construction, providing users with confidence in the quality and reliability of digital assets.

Benchmarking

Benchmarking is defined as the process undertaken at the beginning of a project that determines the settings used in the digitization process so as to ensure that the most significant information is captured by correctly adjusting the resolution or bit depth. The benchmarking approach can be applied across the continuum of digitization, from conversion to presentation. Benchmarking must be approached holistically, and it is essential to understand at the point of selection what the consequences for conversion and presentation will be.

Benchmarking provides a means for interpreting vendors' claims and assists in negotiating with them for services and products. It also leads to careful management of resources. If the requirements of a project are stated up front, a budget can be developed that reflects the actual costs, identifies prerequisites for meeting those needs, and avoids costly mistakes. Benchmarking allows information professionals to be realistic about what can be delivered under specific conditions.

A representative sample of images should be chosen and key features that are critical to the photographs' meaning should be identified. Kenney and Chapman (1996a) state:

> In the rapidly changing technological and information environment, the original document is the least changeable—by defining requirements against it, we can hope to control the circumstances under which digital imaging can satisfy current objectives and meet future needs.... Defining conversion requirements according to curatorial judgments of meaningful document attributes may be the surest guarantee of building digital collections with sufficient richness to be useful for the long-term.

Kenney and Chapman (1996b) continue:

> Determining what constitutes essential detail is a subjective decision that should be made by those with curatorial responsibility and a good understanding of the nature and significance of the material.

> Those with a trained eye should consider the attributes of the
> document itself as well as the potential uses the researchers will
> make of its information content. (26)

Benchmarking is primarily a management tool, designed to lead to
informed decision making about a range of choices and an understanding of the consequences of such judgments. Although actual practice
confirms or modifies decisions, benchmarking reduces experimentation
and the temptation to over- or under-state requirements. It allows
information professionals to scale knowledgeably, making effective
overall decisions rather than developing them individually or setting
requirements that may apply only to a subset of images.

Benchmarking is needed for both in-house and outsourced digitization
projects. An important difference is that with an outsourced project the
prerequisites often have to be formulated before a contract is signed.
In-house projects can devise benchmarking requirements as they
digitize.

Four main parameters when assessing the visual appearance of an
image are spatial resolution, tone reproduction, noise, and color
reproduction. Information professionals can measure and benchmark
these parameters using special targets and software, but visual quality can
be affected by other choices as well. For instance, spatial resolution alone
may be insufficient to produce images as sharp as the original photograph,
tone reproduction is affected by all the components of an imaging system
and is often difficult to control, and color reproduction includes decisions
about pictorial-rendering intent as well as color space and bit depth.
Consider also how visual benchmarks are affected by image processing:
sharpening, filtering, noise reduction, and compression. System evaluation
should encompass subjective visual assessment as well, which requires
that evaluators possessing visual literacy look at the images.

Calibration

Calibration is vital for digitization projects because the range of color
reproduction of different devices varies considerably. The technical
parameters for scanning, impacting on tone reproduction, color
reproduction, spatial resolution, and noise, have to be selected and
systems need to be set up and calibrated carefully. If calibration is done
incorrectly, it results in images that are unacceptable. Ester (1996) states:

If such production steps as color matching present a certain level of complexity in themselves, the prospect of obtaining a consistent collection of images is greatly compounded in difficulty by the many potential junctures for losing control of how images look. Any time an image is captured, changed, or transferred to another system, medium, or device, the outcome may vary from the intended result. The industry is presently at the stage where no transition can be taken for granted. (14)

To reduce the amount of image manipulation required, hardware in the workflow should be calibrated to ensure integrity of color throughout the image capturing process. Frey and Reilly (2006) note:

In many digitization projects monitor calibration is an important consideration, not only when working with images but also when discussing the quality of scans with vendors over the telephone. If monitors are not properly calibrated, the two parties will not see the same image. To solve this potential problem, the National Archives, for example, have the same system setup for their quality control station as their vendor. (32)

Scanner and monitor calibration must be performed regularly, as well as before the beginning of a new project. Scanners are calibrated using the color targets provided with the scanning software. The color management section of the scanning software and monitor must then be properly set to incorporate the scanner profile.

Digital preservation surrogates require quality control, complete documentation of the technical specifications, and calibration of all parts of the digital system, from capture to image display or printed output. Constant calibration can be achieved and maintained when high-resolution images are used within an institution and all elements can be controlled. The quality control and documentation are necessary because it is assumed that the surrogates will outlast the originals, which will continue to deteriorate and will eventually no longer be available to verify the degree to which they are accurately reproduced in the digital images. Complete documentation of the technical specifications is required because it is necessary to approximate the original images as closely as possible in the first place and to verify this relationship perennially, even after the digital image has been migrated a number of times.

Scanning from originals or duplicates

The decision whether to scan from originals or duplicates depends on a number of factors. Quality will always be best if the first generation of an image, such as a negative, is used. However, there may be differences between the negative and the print. Photographers often spend time in the darkroom creating the print, and the results of this work are lost if the negative, rather than the print, is scanned. Scanning a large print with well-executed burning and dodging on an inexpensive flatbed scanner may extract more information than high-resolution scanning from a negative on a costly film scanner. The darkroom manipulations already applied to the print minimize post-scanning work.

Negative collections profit from digitization because it makes them more easily accessible. Negatives are often not used because their image content is unavailable to users. Digitizing glass plate negatives reduces the risk of loss through breakage because they will be handled only once and users can access the digital surrogates.

Batching

Information professionals should calculate the number of scans generated each day based on the speed of the scanner, the resolution of the master files, the efficiency of the scanning technicians, and the speed of the computer processor and network. Moving fragile photographs on and off the scanner is slow, affecting the number of scans generated per day. Retrieving the originals and organizing them in a way that makes digitization as efficient as possible also takes time.

The creation of derivative files should be considered, although this will depend on whether batching software is utilized. Some software packages for image manipulation offer batching procedures that allow users to automatically run a series of alterations to master files and save them in another location. The use of batching tools greatly speeds up the creation of surrogate image files.

Images of the same format, size, complexity, and condition should all be handled in the same way and scanned to one specification. Set-up time per collection, per batch, and per image is a meaningful cost component in digitization. Selection strategies that minimize the differences among the physical attributes of images will streamline digitization workflows.

When considering digital conversion from a hands-on perspective, it is easy to utilize the efficiencies of similar photographs whenever possible. For batch processing to work, the images need to be similar, ideally originating from the same roll of film. Unfortunately, cultural heritage materials are often heterogeneous, so batching may be impossible with many collections. If the images themselves cannot be grouped in like categories, then work should be structured in a series of steps where specific tasks can be conducted for uninterrupted periods. With appropriate configurations, information professionals can break the repetitive cycle of a single task, such as scanning, by moving to another, such as metadata creation. Regular changes of task will facilitate high production and help to ensure consistent quality.

Postproduction work

Some postproduction work is necessary to obtain surrogate images that closely match the original photograph's color fidelity, detail, sharpness, and tonal range. The amount of processing required is governed by the nature of the project. Automatic processing may be appropriate for batches of homogeneous images, while manual adjustments may be performed on individual rare and valuable images.

Institutions should strive to provide researchers with faithful reproductions of entire original images. Images should be framed and cropped to show the entire image and beyond the image's edges, when appropriate. For negatives, this may mean that each digital image reproduces the item's actual image area, the border on the film that surrounds the image area, and a portion of the background beyond the edge of the film. A similar approach can be followed for prints, such as the entire print, mount, and a portion of the background beyond the mount.

Images may also need to be rotated or de-skewed. Image sharpening may be applied if necessary to increase the match between the image and the original. This process, however, should not be used to overcome defects in the scanner quality or in the proper operation of the equipment, or to increase the apparent resolution beyond the resolution of the original.

Color management must begin with correct scanner operation at the time of capture so that the original scan creates as accurate a representation as possible. The original photograph should be compared to the scanned image under controlled viewing conditions on a color-controlled monitor. Using graphics processing software such as Photoshop, the image may be adjusted so that the colors are a close match. During production, the required adjustment can be noted and run as a batch process. When imaging rare or valuable materials the adjustment can be done on individual images.

File-naming conventions

Tracking and identifying digital images is easier by following logical file-naming conventions. Files move through various servers and content management systems during their life span. Computers are unable by themselves to interpret logical relationships in a collection of images. Therefore, these relationships have to be mirrored in the way the scanned image files are named. Some programs allow only a certain number of characters to be used in file names. File-naming conventions are useful for sorting like objects together in search-and-browse results and for creating a persistent URL for digital surrogates. To ensure identification and consistency across collections, as well as to make processing of the files easier, conventions should be followed when creating file names. Two approaches are usually used: either a scheme that reflects identification numbers already used in an existing cataloging system or the construction of meaningful file names.

Each file created must have a unique name that is independent of its location within a directory structure. At a minimum, file names must combine information as to the item's location, a unique identifier, and a file-type extension. Information to the left of the item identifier refers to location information about the item, such as the collection, folder, or accession number; information to the right of the item identifier provides information about the usage of the file, such as kind and type. File names can also impart information as to what the file is, although this is not a requirement.

File names should be 31 characters or less in length, including the three-letter file format extension; use letters of the alphabet, numbers, hyphens, and underscores; and avoid spaces, punctuation marks, or symbols.

Derivative files have the same file names as their master files, with the addition of a usage indicator that is appended to the item number. Master files require no usage indicator.

If a digital object consists of multiple files, each file name must contain the object's identifier and be appended with a unique sequence number containing enough digits to account for all items in the collection. For example, a directory and file-naming structure could be pharch/rg18_77/0000008.tif for the master file and pharch/rg18_77/0000008d.jpg for the derivative file. The directory name 'pharch' represents photographs in the architectural collection, the subdirectory 'rg18_77' denotes the record group 18 and series 77, and the file name represents the eighth photograph scanned.

Quality assessment

Quality control is an important component in each stage of a digital imaging project in order to guarantee the integrity and consistency of the image files. The conditions for digital image quality require the desired end result and production goals to be identified. The quality of the captured image cannot be any better than the source image of a scan; the source image dictates the upper limit of image quality. Different source media have varying scanning requirements. Information professionals should define acceptable levels of digital image quality, based on the attributes of the source image and the capability of the digital imaging system to be used, against which the output of the digitization process can be judged.

Although quality control is a crucial factor in ensuring the best results, there is no standard way to ensure a certain image quality at capture. Different source images require different scanning processes, and this has to be considered when developing a quality control program. Frey and Reilly (2006) note that "There are no guidelines or accepted standards for determining the level of image quality required in the creation of digital image databases for photographic collections" (1). Ester (1995) writes:

> If I see shortcomings in what we are doing in documenting images, they are traceable to the lack of standards in this area. We have responded to a practical need in our work, and have settled on the information we believe is important to record about production and the resulting image resource. These recording procedures have become stable over time, but the data would become even more valuable if there was broad community consensus on a preferred framework. Compatibility of image data from multiple sources and the potential to develop software around access to a common framework would be some of the advantages. (148)

Quality control is implemented by controlling the scanning environment, including hardware, software, and viewing conditions; establishing clear production procedures to ensure that consistent digital objects are created before beginning production; testing procedures and settings to verify that the digital images meet benchmark requirements; and reviewing output to ensure consistent results.

Decisions about quality control include defining the percentage of images that will be evaluated; choosing the methodology for evaluation; controlling the environment for quality control, including configuring the hardware; evaluating system performance; documenting procedures and creating an inspection form; and performing the assessment itself. Evaluation guidelines should be built into the project documentation so that images created in the future meet the same standards and are developed according to the same practices as the originals.

A quality-review process is necessary for both in-house and outsourced images. In both cases, information professionals must ensure that images meet project specifications. Contracts with vendors for digitization services generally include provisions for rejection and re-digitization of images that fail to meet specifications, and institutions contracting with vendors must have a means of identifying these images quickly and accurately. When derivative images are received from the vendor, these too should be subjected to quality review.

The quality control of image files can be maintained by determining an appropriate percentage of images to check, and this will be dependent on the size of the project and the skill of the scanning technician. Bearing in mind the limitations of time and finances, many projects use sampling so as to reduce the costs of this process, such as checking only 10 percent of digital images. The quality review process should be conducted by people other than those performing the digitizing. Reviewing a reasonably sized sample of images allows for the discovery of problems and identifies recurring errors. Ideally, quality control should be performed on all master and derivative images.

Having a complete quality review process in place is no substitute for adequate training and ongoing supervision of digitizing staff. It will also be effective only if image specifications have been well defined and tested at the start of the project, based on a thorough understanding of the source material and digital imaging best practices. Similarly, all imaging devices should be thoroughly tested and profiled frequently throughout the duration of imaging projects.

A histogram, a common tool found in most image processing software packages, may be one way to perform quality assessment. The histogram is a graphic representation of the distribution of gray shades in an image. The height of each vertical line is proportional to the number of pixels of that shade: the taller the line, the more pixels of that shade. The histogram provides indications of certain types of image defects, such as loss of tones in the shadows or highlights of an image.

Metadata has a central role in processing, managing, accessing, and preserving digital collections. Because of the crucial role it plays in the life cycle of collections, metadata review should also be an integral part of a quality control program. Metadata quality control can be done via system checks or manually, or by a combination of these two.

Management systems for images

Image management systems are physical and intellectual systems for managing and accessing images and other digital assets, providing secure storage, arrangement, and management of digital assets for both access and preservation. They record the storage location of master images and derivatives, search for and retrieve images, and provide an access interface, frequently via the internet or a web-based interface. Additionally, they provide contextual or structural frameworks for the digital images, such as associated finding aids and table of contents, respectively.

Using open systems architecture as much as possible is the best method to ensure system viability over time. Open architecture means that the system's components use standards and specifications that have been made public by their designers, which will minimize the impact of incompatibility. Since changes in technology and standards make migration an inevitable part of the life cycle of projects, collections, and objects, files will be migrated to new formats and systems. Although the particulars of such changes cannot be anticipated, the preservation of a high-quality digital master is the best guarantee against the necessity of future re-digitization. The inevitability of migration is one of the reasons why it is essential that digital objects and associated metadata adhere, as much as possible, to widely accepted standards. Technical staff can upgrade hardware and software with minimal impact on the overall system and without significant risk of data loss. Thus, the integrity of the system is more likely to be ensured by using open systems architecture.

Information professionals can choose digital asset management systems (DAMS), which are usually used commercially, or content management systems (CMS), which have evolved in the cultural heritage

Box 6.6   Best practices for content management systems

- Plan a dynamic system that can provide access for continual correction and updating of metadata.

- If open source software is used, be sure there are sufficient development resources to customize the system appropriately.

- Organize the scanned image files into a hierarchy that logically maps to the physical organization of the images.

- Name the scanned files in a strictly controlled manner that reflects their logical relationships.

sector. Both types of system have the ability to manage digital assets, but each has different goals. CMS are concerned with the management of collections and all other work related to collection objects, which means almost all departments of a cultural heritage institution. In many cases, a CMS maps the complete institutional structure.

In comparison, the potential application areas of DAMS do not include all departments of a heritage institution, but are restricted to areas such as media management and publishing. The strength of DAMS clearly lies in the management of digital assets, providing functions far beyond CMS, such as workflow management.

At present, and presumably in the future, if media management and publishing are essential to an organization, CMS cannot replace DAMS; on the other hand, it seems unlikely that a DAMS will substitute for a CMS. DAMS support only some of the necessary functions of a CMS and in ways that are not customized for the specific professional needs of heritage institutions.

Benefits of digitization

Although digitization initiatives are complex, when they are managed successfully their benefits outweigh the great skills, costs, and time required. Increased and enhanced access, reduced handling of fragile or heavily used analog images, the development of technical infrastructure and staff skills, and opportunities for collaboration and securing funding make digitization worthwhile for institutions embarking on projects of their own.

The appetite for visual material is infinite. The quality of digital image collections will evolve through generous investments of time, effort, and resources. However strong the coverage might be in any given subject, there is always room for improvement—more images, higher-quality digital capture and scanning, and richer data. With academic discourse fanning out into ever more specialized areas of inquiry, image collections will continue to grow exponentially.

The digitization of cultural heritage materials brings together various sectors of the research community in an unprecedented manner. The user groups of traditional library, archives, and museum structures have been redefined by the growing use of the internet. Scholars are creating or using electronic resources to further their research, distance-learning models prompt teachers to gather resources via the web in an online environment, and publishers are integrating print with digital editions to reach wider audiences. The unique properties of the digital medium give visual form to cultural heritage information. The interactive techniques of the internet provide new opportunities for archives, libraries, and museums to develop a global user community to utilize their collections of historical photographs.

7

Conclusion

Through being photographed, something becomes part of a system of information, fitted into schemes of classification and storage.... Reality as such is redefined—as an item for exhibition, as a record for scrutiny, as a target for surveillance. (Susan Sontag, 1977)

Our world has developed such a voracious appetite for information in visual form, and the digital image has such overwhelming technical and economic advantages as a way to meeting this demand, that it seems certain to succeed the photograph as our primary medium of visual record—much as the photograph itself succeeded the hand-drawn and painted image. Unlike silver-based photographic film, the digital image does not consume scarce, nonrenewable resources. It does not require a time-consuming and expensive chemical development process. It can be stored compactly, accessed by computer, manipulated freely, and transmitted to remote locations within seconds of creation. (William J. Mitchell, 2001)

A photograph is a time capsule that extends from the past to the future. (Henry Jesionka)

Since its invention more than 150 years ago, photography has revolutionized communication and has provided a technological method for the comprehensive documentation of social and physical landscapes. Since photographic images serve as immediate links to the past and transcend time and place, they provide a valuable visual record of the past century for scholars and non-academic users alike.

Due to photography's usage as a primary source for pedagogy and research, archives, libraries, and museums holding historical photograph collections have a responsibility to manage them properly and make them available for generations to come. Until the advent of online collections, most historical collections of photography were difficult to access, but as photographic equipment and methods have evolved, so have photographic collections. The digitization of image collections has vastly increased the numbers of images available to researchers through electronic means. The phenomenal growth of digital information in cultural heritage institutions prompts an examination of the nature and importance of hybrid image collections, as technology changes the ways in which users access information and conduct research.

There is a continuing argument within memory institutions and photographic circles that nothing changes with regard to how users evaluate the relevance of a photograph, even if it no longer has a material existence but is stored as digital code. Users continue to view images, whether analog or digital, as indexical representations of the real. Others feel that digital images are pure abstractions with constitutive mutability and manipulation, and that without some physical link to their subjects, they are not 'real' photographs. The first approach emphasizes the continuity of the medium, based on the unchanging combination of photographer, camera, and subject. Those who see digitization as the end of photography wish to cling to the traditional, tangible imprint of reality; they blame digitization for the death of photography, for the end of the believability that photography holds as an index, rather than an icon or symbol.

How the nature of photography has changed as a result of digitization remains a matter of discussion. As Batchen (1999) notes:

> A singular point of origin, a definitive meaning, a linear narrative: all of these traditional historical props are henceforth displaced from photography's provenance. In their place we have discovered something far more provocative—a way of rethinking photography that persuasively accords with the medium's undeniable conceptual, political, and historical complexity. (202)

Whatever the conclusion to this debate, it seems clear that digital technology has thoroughly assimilated photography of all kinds, including image collections that will enter the archives, libraries, and museums hereafter. Lipkin (2005) notes that the future holds more questions than answers:

> How will [technological] advances change our notion of what photography can or should be? What will happen as modeling software becomes increasingly capable of generating photo-realistic imagery that cannot be distinguished in any way from real life? The only thing we can be sure of is that the human desire to understand the world through representation will propel the process of making images through greater and greater changes in the years to come. (10)

Although the fate of photography remains unknown, and technical, social, practical, and theoretical issues continue to emerge, there are several factors that information professionals can depend on as they look to the future of image management. Digital resources will increase significantly and information technology will change rapidly. Research trends will expand and scholars will continue to demand that collections be as inclusive as possible. Intellectual property rights management will also evolve as digital content replaces analog sources. Financial and human resources will be unable to keep pace with demand but should be allocated in the most cost-effective manner to achieve an acceptable balance between the quality of resources and the expenditure of time and money. The sustainability of collections will also continue to be an issue, as digitization is not just about the creation of images, but also about their maintenance and management. As a result of these developments, best practices for access, preservation, and management of image collections will transform as well.

The aim of *Managing Image Collections: A practical guide* has been to explain the historical, cultural, and technological context of hybrid image collections, with particular reference to issues concerning the heritage sector. By understanding and embracing the technological shift in the production of photographs, while still maintaining traditional, analog images, information professionals will be best informed in their ability to create, maintain, and deliver quality image collections of enduring value in a dynamic information environment.

Appendix A:
Digital project considerations

Audience

Who is the intended audience?

Are they specialists, general users, or both?

What are the needs of the users, and how can they be best served?

What will digitization enable them to do that is not possible with analog images?

Selection

Do the images reflect the institutional mission and collections policies?

What is the intellectual value of such images and their informational content?

What are the images that are most valuable for teaching and scholarship?

What images are used most frequently, and how are they used?

What images are unique to the institution?

Do the images have sufficient intrinsic value to ensure interest in their digital surrogates?

Will digitization significantly enhance access or increase use by an identifiable constituency?

How much of the collection is well documented?

What images are of highest monetary value?

What images are judged to be at highest risk, and why?

Are there any restricted or sensitive images to be excluded?

Are the images well captioned?

Will the proposed scanning technique be able to capture the appearance of the item accurately?

Will disparate collections be unified?

Are the images duplicated well elsewhere?

Do the selected images accurately represent the collection's strengths?

Is there a danger of over- or under-representing specific themes?

Physical characteristics of collection

How many items have to be digitized?

What are the formats of the collection?

What is the physical condition of the images?

How will the originals need to be handled during scanning in order to prevent damage?

Will the images be able to withstand handling during the scanning process?

What are the sizes of the images? Are they oversized?

Intellectual property rights and legal and cultural considerations

Who will be responsible for evaluating the copyright status of selected images?

Who owns the rights to the images?

Are they in the public domain? If not, can permissions be secured?

Are there legal or cultural considerations to be addressed?

Are the images free from donor restrictions that would prevent them from being digitized or publicly accessed?

Funding

Who will be responsible for fundraising and grant writing?

What are the funding sources?

Who will manage budgets?

What parts of the project will funding support?

Are the costs in line with the anticipated value?

Are the costs of scanning and post-scan processing supportable?

What will it cost to maintain access into the future?

Technology

Is there sufficient technical infrastructure to create, manage, and deliver digital projects?

Does current technology yield image quality adequate to meet project goals?

What hardware is required to meet digitization needs?

What software is required to meet digitization needs?

Are there sufficient storage facilities to meet digitization needs?

Project planning

What will be the short-term, immediate benefits of the project?

What will be the long-term, strategic benefits of the project?

What are the expected outcomes of the project?

What is the intended workflow of the project?

Staffing

Does the institution have the necessary expertise and resources to plan and implement the project?

What skills, experience, or training will be required for each activity?

Who will oversee digitization initiatives?

What kind of staff are needed, and what will their responsibilities be?

What institutional support and leadership can they expect?

How will digitization affect staff roles and service at the institution?

Are staff levels and available skills appropriate to support the growing size and scope of the collections and access to these images by users?

Who will be responsible for each stage of digitization?

Who will write project documentation and progress reports?

Preparation

Will images be conserved before being scanned?

Will it be necessary to clean images prior to scanning?

Will images need to be encapsulated or de-encapsulated prior to scanning?

Will images need to be transported before digitization?

Digitization

Will the digitizing be done in-house or contracted to a vendor?

What are the resolutions and bit depths needed?

Will the files be compressed?

Should the images be faithful reproductions or optimized for presentation?

How will copies of the images be stored?

Are there specific image guidelines specified by the funding source?

Will master and derivative files be created?

Quality assessment

Is digitization complete? Are images missing?

Have the file-naming conventions been adhered to?

Are the files named for the correct original images?

Have the images been captured in the correct mode (color or grayscale)?

Are the images in the correct format and, if appropriate, are the compression ratios correct?

Are the resolutions and bit depths correct?

Are the tonal values and color balances correct?

Are the brightness and contrast settings correct?

Are there noticeable interference, noise, or artifacts?

Does the image accurately represent the qualities of the original?

Have the significant details been successfully reproduced?

Have the images been checked on a variety of monitors?

If printing is required, have the images been output to a variety of printers?

Description and metadata

Who uses the images and how do they request photographs?

What are the most frequently requested subjects?

What type of description already exists for the collection?

At what level will metadata be recorded: item, collection, or both?

Is there sufficient metadata available to match perceived user needs and project aims?

What metadata or finding aid schema will be used?

If there are several versions of an original, which version will be cataloged?

Is it possible to create metadata that satisfies both general and specialized users?

What level of granularity will most likely benefit users?

Are other data fields necessary as access points that might be of interest to users?

Will extensive research time be required to record even the minimal metadata required?

Is there enough information readily available about the images to provide a useful context for potential audiences?

Access

Will the images be linked to existing systems, or will it be necessary to develop a new access method for the images?

At what level will access be provided: item, collection, or both?

Will the images be accessible and deliverable online?

How will users locate the collections, items within the collections, and relevant subsets of the items?

How will images be viewed? One at a time, or several together so as to facilitate comparisons?

Will zooming be required?

Will access be appropriately controlled?

Time frame

What are the critical deadlines?

How long will each component of the project take?

What are the anticipated start and end dates?

Does the time frame include the possibility of delays?

Collaboration and outreach

Will the project have a collaborative component?

Is the collaboration local, national, or international?

Is there a community outreach component?

What will the instructional and end-user support be?

Content management systems

What new opportunities is the CMS intended to create?

How will institutional buy-in be ensured?

What is the cost-benefit ratio?

What is the anticipated impact of the CMS on organizational thinking about and use of digital content?

How will the CMS technology be integrated into existing systems?

What metadata will be required to support the application of CMS technology?

Evaluation

How will evaluation of the digital resources be undertaken?

What measures exist to demonstrate that the project has succeeded?

How will user perceptions and expectations of the project be addressed?

Sustainability

How and where will be the archival images be stored?

What kind of backup mechanisms are in place in case of hardware or software failure?

What are the data migration and refreshment plans?

Is demonstrable long-term support in place to maintain the project and ensure its longevity in the future?

Appendix B:
Glossary of image collection terms

access image: *see* surrogate image.

additive color: three colors (red, green, and blue) used in the additive process of color photography. When added together, they produce white. Also called additive primary.

additive primary: *see* additive color.

administrative metadata: metadata retained to track the creation and maintenance of digital objects.

albumen: the white of an egg, used as a carrier for silver salts in nineteenth-century photographic prints and plates.

aliasing: the visual stair-stepping of edges that occurs in images when the resolution is too low.

ambrotype: a slightly underexposed collodion wet-plate glass negative displayed in a frame backed by black material.

analog: information available by continuously variable physical means, in contrast to digital means.

anti-alias: a technique where neighboring pixels are blended to reduce the stair-stepping effect often found along diagonal edges and lines.

archival image: *see* master image.

artifact: a visual effect unintentionally introduced into a digital image in the course of digitizing or during imaging software manipulation.

autochrome: a colored, transparent image on glass, similar to a slide, created by a layer of dyed potato starch.

banding: a visible stair stepping of shades in a gradient.

bandwidth: the amount of data that can pass through a given channel at one time.

base: the support that carries a photosensitive emulsion. Photographic films use a transparent base; photographic prints use an opaque base, usually paper.

batch scanning: sequential scanning of multiple originals using previously defined settings.

Bayer pattern: a pattern of red, green, and blue filters on the image sensor. Because the human eye is more sensitive to green, there are twice as many green filters as blue and red filters.

binary code: a system of encoding data that uses 0 and 1.

binder: the transparent layer on a photograph in which the final image is suspended.

bit: the smallest unit of computer data, denoted by a single binary value, either 0 or 1.

bit depth: a measurement of the number of bits used to represent each pixel in a digital image. Also called color depth or dynamic range.

bitmap: the method of storing information that maps pixels, bit by bit.

bitmapped image: an image created from a series of bits that form pixels. Also called raster image.

bitonal: images that are restricted to black and white values.

blur: lack of sharpness, usually at the edges of light and dark areas of images.

boilerplate text: standardized text used for digital files.

born digital: images or documents that were originally created or captured in digital form.

brightness: the balance of light and dark shades in images.

byte: a unit of data that is eight bits long.

C-type print: a color process with at least three emulsion layers of light-sensitive silver salts.

cabinet card: an albumen silver print, popular in the nineteenth century, mounted on a card measuring approximately 6½ inches by 4¼ inches.

calibration: the act of adjusting the color of one device relative to another or one device to an established standard.

calotype: a photographic process in which paper sensitized with silver salts is used in a camera to produce paper negatives. Also called talbotype.

camera lucida: Latin for 'light room.' An instrument using a prism or mirrors to cause an image of an object to be projected upon a surface to be traced.

camera obscura: Latin for 'dark room.' Originally a dark room with a small hole in one side that formed images on the opposite wall, it was later developed into a portable box with a lens that formed an image on tracing paper for hand copying.

carbon print: a photographic print formed by a pigmented gelatin layer on a paper support.

carte-de-visite: an albumen silver print, popular in the nineteenth century, mounted on a card measuring approximately 4½ inches by 2½ inches.

CCD (charge-coupled device): light-sensitive diodes used in scanners and digital cameras that, when exposed to light, generate digital signals that are converted into pixel values.

charge-coupled device: *see* CCD.

Cibachrome: *see* Ilfochrome.

CMOS (complementary metal oxide semiconductor): a sensor similar to CCD that uses negative and positive polarity circuits.

CMS (color management system): a system that ensures color uniformity across input and output devices so that the final printed results match the original.

CMY (cyan, magenta, yellow): the primary colors of the subtractive color model.

CMYK (cyan, magenta, yellow, black): a subtractive color model used in four-color printing.

collection: a group of objects that, when considered as a whole, demonstrates some identifiable organizing principle.

collodion: a transparent material made of guncotton (nitrocellulose) dissolved in ether and alcohol, used as a carrier for light-sensitive silver salts in the wet-plate process.

color balance: the ability of photographic materials to reproduce colors accurately.

color depth: *see* bit depth.

color gamut: the range of colors that can be displayed, printed, or captured by a particular monitor, film, printer, scanner, or other device.

color management: technology that translates the colors of a given color space to the color space of an output device.

color management system: *see* CMS.

complementary metal oxide semiconductor: *see* CMOS.

compression: the re-encoding of data to minimize disk space and transmission time over networks.

continuous tone: photographic images that contain full gradation of tonalities.

contrast: the difference in brightness between the lightest and darkest parts of images.

controlled vocabulary: a defined set of words or phrases used to describe objects.

copyright: legal protection provided to authors of original works, including literary, dramatic, musical, artistic, and other intellectual works, published and unpublished.

cropping: to trim the edges of images.

crosswalk: a mapping of the elements, semantics, and syntax from one metadata schema to another.

cyanotype: a photographic process, in monochromatic blue, using light-sensitive iron salts.

daguerreotype: a photographic process that uses a silver surface sensitized with iodine and developed by exposure to mercury vapor.

data: a reinterpretable representation of information in a formalized manner suitable for communication, interpretation, or processing.

database: a set of data usually stored in one location and made available to several users at the same time for various applications.

definition: the clarity of detail in images affected by resolution and contrast.

density: the relative difference between the lightest and darkest parts of an image.

depth of field: the range of distances along the axis of a camera lens through which an object will produce a relatively distinct image.

derivative image: *see* surrogate image.

descriptive metadata: metadata primarily intended to serve the purposes of discovery, identification, and selection.

developing-out paper (DOP): a sensitized printing paper requiring development in order to bring out the image.

digital: information available in electronic form, readable by computer, in contrast to analog form.

digital camera: a device that records data in pixels, rather than on film.

digital capture: using a scanner, digital camera, or other device to create a digital representation of an object.

digital object: the digital representation of an analog counterpart, consisting of data, metadata, and an identifier.

digital preservation: the process of maintaining accessibility of digital objects over time.

digitization: the conversion from paper, film, or other media formats to an electronic format.

diodes: light-sensitive electronic components used by scanners or digital cameras during image capture.

direct positive: a positive obtained from another positive without an intermediate step.

DOP: *see* developing-out paper.

dots per inch: *see* dpi.

downsampling: a technique for reducing the amount of digital data used to represent images.

dpi (dots per inch): a measurement of the scanning resolution of images or the quality of an output device.

drum scanner: a high-quality image-capture device in which the image is wrapped around a drum that spins while a light source scans across it.

dry plate: a glass photographic plate that is used dry, differentiated from the wet-plate process, which it superseded.

Dublin Core: an officially recognized international metadata standard with fifteen elements, designed principally by the library and archives community, to manage the description of information resources, particularly web content.

dye destruction print: a photographic process with at least three emulsion layers, each one sensitized to a different primary color (red, blue or green) and each one containing a dye related to that color.

dye transfer print: a complex form of early color printing in which a color transparency was photographed three times, in each case through a different filter.

dynamic range: *see* bit depth.

emulation: a digital preservation strategy that uses current software to simulate original or obsolete computer environments.

emulsion: the light-sensitive layer of film or paper.

encryption: the process of encoding data so that only authorized users are able to convert the data back to its original encoding for presentation.

evidential value: the value of records in providing authentic and reliable information on decisions, actions, transactions, and communications made by the organization that created the records.

ferrotype: *see* tintype.

file extension: letters appearing after the dot at the end of a filename to help the computer identify the file format and what software should be used to interpret it.

file size: the amount of computer storage space a file requires, usually measured in kilobytes or megabytes.

film: material used in cameras to record photographic images, generally a light-sensitive emulsion coated on a flexible acetate or plastic base.

film base: a flexible support on which light-sensitive emulsion is coated.

film scanner: a device that scans slides and negatives to create digital images.

flatbed scanner: a device on which the original image remains stationary while sensors pass over or under it.

GB: *see* gigabyte.

gelatin silver print: a standard contemporary monochrome print in which the paper is treated with the same gelatin silver emulsion used in the gelatin dry-plate process.

GIF (Graphic Interchange Format): an image file format suitable for storing graphics with relatively few colors, such as diagrams, logos, and animation.

gigabyte (GB): a unit of memory or file size that equals 1,024 megabytes.

grain: a granular texture visible under magnification in processed silver halide emulsions, a result of the clumping of silver particles during processing.

granularity: the level of detail in a metadata record.

Graphic Interchange Format: *see* GIF.

grayscale: images that use black, white, and a range of gray shades.

gum-bichromate process: a photographic printing process that is dependent upon the hardening effect of light on gum arabic mixed with potassium dichromate. Also called gum-dichromate process or gum process.

gum-dichromate process: *see* gum-bichromate process.

gum process: *see* gum-bichromate process.

halftone: a process for representing the tones in an image by dots of varying sizes.

heliograph: a photographic process using pewter plates coated with bitumen of Judea and washed with a solvent.

histogram: a graphical representation of the tonal values in images based upon the frequency of occurrence of each value.

Ilfochrome: a process by which a photographic print is made directly from a color transparency. Also called Cibachrome.

image: a representation of subject matter in analog and digital form.

image processing: any operation that can be performed on digital data to alter its characteristics and thereby the image that it represents.

informational value: the secondary value of records for reference and research, derived from the information contained in them, and may be incidental to their original purpose.

inkjet print: the most common form of printing digital files onto paper using a technology that sprays droplets of ink onto the paper.

interoperability: the ability of multiple systems, using different hardware and software platforms, data structures, and interfaces to exchange data.

interpolation: a process of increasing resolution by the addition of new pixels throughout the image.

IRIS print: a color print combining fine-art print making and computerized imaging techniques on a high-quality inkjet printer.

item: a single physical object, the basic unit of arrangement and description within an archival series.

Joint Photographic Experts Group: *see* JPEG.

JPEG (Joint Photographic Experts Group): an image file format which commonly uses a method of lossy compression.

KB: *see* kilobyte.

kilobyte (KB): a unit of computer memory or data storage capacity equal to 1,024 bytes.

Kodachrome: the first commercially successful integral tripack color process using dyes incorporated into silver-gelatin emulsions.

lantern slide: an image on glass used in early slide projectors to project photographs to an audience.

latent image: an image formed by the changes to the silver halide grains in photographic emulsion on exposure to light, not visible until chemical development.

lateral reversal: a mirror image where the image is flipped from left to right.

layer: a function of graphics applications in which elements may be isolated from each other, so a group of elements can be manipulated without affecting other elements.

Lempel-Ziv-Welch: *see* LZW.

lithography: a mechanical printing process based on the principle of the natural repulsion of water by grease.

lossless: a file-compression technique for digital objects in which file size is reduced but the information in the original file is recoverable.

lossy: a file compression technique for digital objects in which the information removed is unrecoverable.

LZW (Lempel-Ziv-Welch): a proprietary lossless compression algorithm.

master image: a high-resolution image that contains the greatest fidelity to the original, from which derivative images are created. Also called archival image.

MB: *see* megabyte.

MP: *see* megapixel.

megabyte (MB): a unit of computer memory or data storage capacity equal to 1,048,576 bytes.

megapixel (MP): one million pixels, used as a unit of resolution for digital cameras.

melainotype: *see* tintype.

metadata: structured information that describes digital objects.

metadata schema: a set of metadata elements and rules for their use that has been defined for a particular purpose.

migration: a digital preservation technique used to preserve the integrity of digital files by transferring them across hardware and software configurations and subsequent generations of computer technology.

modern photographic print: contemporary print made from an old original negative.

moiré pattern: an undesirable pattern in printed photographs or halftone images that commonly occurs when two screens are overlapped, such as when scanning a previously offset-printed picture.

negative: a photographic image in which tonalities and colors are reversed from the original image, usually used to make a positive print.

noise: extraneous data introduced into digital objects in the course of digitization and that are due to imperfections or sensitivities in the capture device.

OCR: *see* optical character recognition.

oil print: a photographic process in which paper coated with bichromated gelatin is exposed under a negative, immersed in water, and dried, which makes the surface of the print receptive to color oil pigments, applied by hand.

open standards: freely available structures, procedures, or tools for the uniform creation and description of data.

optical character recognition (OCR): a computer method for converting scanned pages of text into an electronic document.

photogram: a photographic image produced without a camera by placing an object on a sensitized surface and exposing it to light.

photography: a process designed to produce images by means of chemical changes initiated by light.

photogravure: a photomechanical process that uses etched metal plates to provide high-quality reproductions of photographs in ink.

photomechanical reproduction: the duplication of photographs or other graphic material in ink by means of photosensitive plates used on printing presses.

photomontage: the technique of combining one or more photographs to produce a new image.

pinhole camera: a basic camera, in which light is introduced into a darkened box via a small aperture.

pixel: derived from 'picture element,' the smallest element of data of a digitized image.

pixel dimensions: horizontal and vertical measurements of an image expressed in pixels.

pixels per inch: *see* ppi.

pixilation: an undesirable effect caused by images with too low a resolution, producing edges with a stair stepped effect.

platinotype: *see* platinum print process.

platinum print process: a photographic print process based on light-sensitive iron salts, which form an image of platinum metal in the finished print. Also called platinotype.

PNG (Portable Network Graphics): image file format created as the free, open-source successor to the GIF.

Polaroid: an instant film, giving an almost immediate positive print.

POP: *see* printing-out paper.

Portable Network Graphics: *see* PNG.

positive: an image with the same tonal relationships as the subject.

ppi (pixels per inch): the resolution achieved by using a scanner or digital camera.

preservation: specific measures, individual and collective, undertaken to maintain, repair, restore, or protect records.

preservation metadata: information captured to ensure the long-term retention and preservation of a digital object.

print: a photographic image on an opaque base, usually paper.

printing-out paper (POP): a printing paper that does not require development, but produces a visible image directly from exposure.

provenance: the history of ownership of materials prior to acquisition by the current institution.

public domain: a term or concept used to define works in which copyright or intellectual property rights have expired, or which are not covered by intellectual property rights.

quality control: techniques used to ensure that high quality is maintained through the various stages of digitization.

raster image: *see* bitmapped image.

RAW: an image file format created by a digital camera or scanner to be processed and modified to produce a TIFF or JPEG file.

refreshing: a digital preservation technique of periodically moving a file from one physical storage medium to another in order to avoid the obsolescence or degradation of the storage medium.

resampling: changing the resolution of a bitmap without changing the file size.

resolution: the number of pixels, in both height and width, composing an image. The more pixels, the higher the resolution; the higher the resolution, the greater its clarity and definition and the greater the file size.

retouching: the correction of technical flaws or alteration of a photograph for aesthetic reasons, by hand techniques or computer.

RGB (red, green, blue): the three primary colors for additive color mixing, used in televisions, computer monitors, and stage lighting.

salted-paper print: a photographic process using light-sensitive salts soaked into uncoated paper, which is then sensitized with silver nitrate and exposed under a negative.

sampling: the process in which an image is divided into regularly spaced components and its values are measured and converted into binary code.

saturation: the vividness or purity of a color.

scanner: a device for capturing analog images as digital data.

silver halide: a chemical compound of silver used as the light-sensitive constituent in films.

slide: a transparency, often a positive image in color, mounted between glass or in a frame of cardboard or other material so that it may be inserted into a projector.

stereograph: a matched pair of photographs made simultaneously with a camera and which, when viewed, appear as a three-dimensional image.

stereoscope: a binocular device the creates the illusion of three dimensions when viewing a stereograph.

stock images: images available from a commercial source that can be used for a fee.

structural metadata: information that describes the organization of a digital object.

substrate: the material on which an image is printed, usually paper.

subtractive color: three colors (cyan, yellow, and magenta) used in the subtractive process of color photography. When added together, they produce black. Also called subtractive primary.

subtractive primary: *see* subtractive color.

surrogate image: a digital image created from a master image, usually involving sampling to a lower resolution or using lossy compression techniques. Also called an access image or a derivative image.

Tagged Image File Format: *see* TIFF.

talbotype: *see* calotype.

technical metadata: information that describes the technical properties of a specific digital object type.

thumbnail: a proxy image, scaled to a small size, used to represent the original image in circumstances where loading the original is undesirable.

TIFF (Tagged Image File Format): an image file format that is a widely accepted standard in publishing.

tintype: a variation of the wet-plate process, in which the collodion emulsion is coated on a black-lacquered metal sheet and exposed directly in the camera. When viewed in the proper light, the resulting silver image appears as a positive. Also called ferrotype or melainotype.

transparency: a positive image on a transparent base, such as film or glass, viewed by transmitted, rather than reflected, light.

upsampling: a technique for increasing the amount of digital data used to represent images.

vector graphics: images defined using coordinate points and mathematically drawn lines and curves, which may be freely scaled and rotated without image degradation.

vintage photographic print: an image printed around the same time as the negative was made.

watermark: a pattern of bits inserted into a digital file that identifies the file's copyright information.

wet-plate process: a photographic process in which glass or metal plates are coated with collodion, sensitized by being dipped in silver nitrate solution, exposed in a camera, and developed before the collodion can dry.

woodburytype: a photomechanical technique for high-quality reproduction of photographs in ink that is dependent upon the hardening action of light on a gelatin layer. A relief pattern is produced that is then transferred to lead plates for inking and printing.

Appendix C: Further reading

Print resources

History of photography

Braive, M. F. (1966). *The photograph: A social history*. New York: McGraw-Hill.

Coke, V. D. (1972). *The painter and the photograph from Delacroix to Warhol*. Albuquerque, NM: University of New Mexico Press.

Daval, J.-L. (1982). *Photography: History of an art*. New York: Rizzoli.

Freund, G. (1980). *Photography and society*. Boston, MA: David R. Godine.

Frizot, M. (Ed.) (1998). *A new history of photography*. Cologne: Könemann.

Gernsheim, H. and Gernsheim, A. (1969). *The history of photography from the camera obscura to the beginning of the modern era*. New York: McGraw-Hill.

Hambourg, M. M. (1993). *The waking dream: Photography's first century: Selections from the Gilman Paper Company collection*. New York: Metropolitan Museum of Art.

LeMagny, J.-C. and Rouillé, A. (Eds.) (1987). *A history of photography*. New York: Cambridge University Press.

Moholy, L. (1939). *A hundred years of photography*. London: Penguin.

Newhall, B. (1964). *The history of photography: From 1839 to the present*. New York: Museum of Modern Art.

Rosenblum, N. (2007). *A world history of photography*. New York: Abbeville.

Scharf, A. (1974). *Art and photography*. Harmondsworth, Middlesex: Penguin.

Szarkowski, J. (1989). *Photography until now*. Springs of achievement series on the art of photography. New York: Museum of Modern Art.

Weaver, M. and Wolf, D. (1989). *The art of photography, 1839–1989*. New Haven, CT: Yale University Press.

Nineteenth-century photography

Bann, S. (2001). *Parallel lines: Printmakers, painters and photographers in nineteenth-century France*. New Haven, CT: Yale University Press.

Bartram, M. (1985). *The Pre-Raphaelite camera*. New York: New York Graphic Society.

Batchen, G. (1999). *Burning with desire: The conception of photography*. Cambridge, MA: MIT Press.

Buerger, J. E. (1989). *French daguerreotypes*. Chicago: University of Chicago.

Carlebach, M. L. (1992). *The origins of photojournalism in America*. Washington, DC: Smithsonian Institution Press.

Galassi, P. (1981). *Before photography: Painting and the invention of photography*. New York: Museum of Modern Art.

Hamilton, P. and Hargreaves, R. (2001). *The beautiful and the damned: The creation of identity in nineteenth century photography*. London: Lund Humphries in association with the National Portrait Gallery.

Rudisill, R. (1971). *Mirror image: The influence of the daguerreotype on American society*. Albuquerque, NM: University of New Mexico Press.

Sandweisss, M. A. (Ed.) (1991). *Photography in nineteenth-century America*. New York: Harry N. Abrams.

Seiberling, G. (1986). *Amateurs, photography, and the mid-Victorian imagination*. Chicago: University of Chicago Press.

Thomas, A. (1977). *Time in a frame: Photography and the 19th-century mind*. New York: Schocken Books.

Contemporary photography

Bright, S. (2005). *Art photography now*. New York: Aperture.

Campany, D. (Ed.) (2003). *Art and photography*. London: Phaidon.

Cotton, C. (2004). *The photograph as contemporary art*. London: Thames & Hudson.

Doss, E. (Ed.) (2001). *Looking at Life Magazine*. Washington, DC: Smithsonian Institution Press.

Howarth, S. (Ed.) (2005). *Singular images: Essays on remarkable photographs*. New York: Aperture.

Kemper, S. (1998). *Virtual anxiety: Photography, new technologies, and subjectivity*. Manchester: Manchester University Press.

Mitchell, W. (2001). *The reconfigured eye: Visual truth in the post-photographic era*. Cambridge, MA: MIT Press.

Technical guides

Kipphan, H. (2001). *Handbook of print media: Technologies and production methods*. New York: Springer.

Peres, M. R. (2008). *The concise Focal encyclopedia of photography: From the first photo on paper to the digital revolution*. Burlington, MA: Focal Press/Elsevier.

Photographic theory and criticism

Barthes, R. (1981). *Camera lucida: Reflections on photography*. New York: Hill and Wang.

Berger, J. (1972). *Ways of seeing*. New York: Penguin Books.

Bolton, R. (Ed.) (1989). *The contest of meaning: Critical histories of photography*. Cambridge, MA: MIT Press.

Burgin, V. (Ed.) (1982). *Thinking photography*. London: Macmillan.

Evans, J. (Ed.) (1997). *The camerawork essays*. London: Rivers Oram Press.

Solomon-Godeau, A. (1991). *Photography at the dock: Essays on photographic history, institutions, and practices*. Minneapolis, MN: University of Minnesota Press.

Sontag, S. (1977). *On photography*. New York: Farrar, Straus and Giroux.

Wells, L. (Ed.) (2003). *The photography reader*. London: Routledge.

Wells, L. (Ed.) (2009). *Photography: A critical introduction*. London: Routledge.

Photographic formats

Coe, B. and Haworth-Booth, M. (1983). *A guide to early photographic processes*. London: Hurtwood Press.

Crawford, W. (1979). *The keepers of light: A history and working guide to early photographic processes*. Dobbs Ferry, NY: Morgan and Morgan.

Darrah, W. C. (1964). *Stereoviews: A history of stereographs in America and their collection*. Gettysburg, PA: William Culp Darrah.

Morgan, H. and Brown, A. (1981). *Prairie fires and paper moons: The American photograph postcard: 1900–1920*. Boston, MA: D. R. Godine.

Oliver, B. (2006). *A history of the Woodburytype: The first successful photomechanical printing process and Walter Bentley Woodbury*. Nevada City, CA: Carl Mautz.

Reilly, J. M. (1986). *Care and identification of 19th-century photographic prints*. Rochester, NY: Eastman Kodak.

Sutcliffe, G. (1995). *Slide collection management in libraries and information units*. Brookfield, VT: Gower.

Valverde, M. F. (2003). *Photographic negatives: Nature and evolution of processes*. Rochester, NY: Image Permanence Institute.

Ware, M. (1999). *Cyanotype: The history, science and art of photographic printing in Prussian blue*. London: Science Museum.

Format identification

Baldwin, G. and Jürgens, M. C. (2009). *Looking at photographs: A guide to technical terms*. Los Angeles: J. Paul Getty Museum.

Gascoigne, B. (2004). *How to identify prints: A complete guide to manual and mechanical processes from woodcut to ink jet*. New York: Thames & Hudson.

Color photography

Coe, B. (1978). *Colour photography: The first hundred years, 1840–1940*. London: Ash and Grant.

Coote, J. H. (1993). *The illustrated history of colour photography*. Surbiton: Fountain Press.

Rijper, E. (2002). *Kodachrome: The American invention of our world, 1939–1959*. New York: Delano Greenidge Editions.

Conservation of analog photographs

Eaton, G. T. (1985). *Conservation of photographs*. Kodak Publication F-40. Rochester, NY: Eastman Kodak Company.

Lavédrine, B., Gandolfo, J.-P., and Monod, S. (2003). *A guide to the preventative conservation of photograph collections*. Los Angeles: Getty Conservation Institute.

McCabe, C. (2005). *Coatings on photographs: Materials, techniques, and conservation*. Washington, DC: American Institute for Conservation.

Online resources

Photography timelines

Image Permanence Institute Photography Timeline
  www.archivaladvisor.org/shtml/gal_phototimeline.shtml
Photomuse
  http://photomuse.org/chrono.html
Timeline of Color Photography
  www.bu.edu/prc/GODOWSKY/timeline.htm

Overviews of photographic processes

British Library, Historic Photographs, Photographic Processes
  www.british-library.uk/onlinegallery/features/photographicproject/
  photographicprocesses.html
Lost and Found: Rediscovering Early Photographic Processes
  http://imsc.usc.edu/haptics/LostandFound/welcome.html
Victoria and Albert Museum: Photographic Processes
  www.vam.ac.uk/vastatic/microsites/photography/processes.php

Photographic formats

Albumen: Albumen Photographs: History, Science and Preservation
  http://albumen.stanford.edu
Art of the Photogravure
  www.photogravure.com/history/chapter_introduction.html
The Making of a Daguerreotype
  www.daguerre.org/resource/exhibit/brochure.htm
The Stereoscopic Association
  www.stereoscopicsociety.org.uk/

Searchable image collections

America's First Look into the Camera: Daguerreotype Portraits and
   Views, 1838–1864
   http://memory.loc.gov/ammem/daghtml
The American Museum of Photography
   www.photographymuseum.com
Early Photography: 1839–1860
   www.earlyphotography.nl/indexonload2.htm
George Eastman House
   www.geh.org
The Getty
   www.getty.edu
Library of Congress' Photostream on Flickr
   www.flickr.com/photos/library_of_congress/
Library of Congress: Prints and Photographs Online Catalog
   www.loc.gov/pictures/
Museum of Contemporary Photography
   www.mocp.org
New York Public Library Digital Gallery: Photography Collection
   http://digitalgallery.nypl.org/nypldigital

General digitization guides

Best Practice Guidelines for Digital Collections, University of Maryland
   Libraries
   www.lib.umd.edu/dcr/publications/best_practice.pdf
A Framework of Guidance for Building Good Digital Collections
   http://framework.niso.org/
The NINCH Guide to Good Practice in the Digital Representation and
   Management of Cultural Heritage Materials
   www.nyu.edu/its/humanities/ninchguide/
Visual Arts Data Service's Creating Digital Resources for the Visual
   Arts: Standards and good practice
   http://vads.ahds.ac.uk/guides/creating_guide/contents.html
Washington State Library Digital Best Practices
   http://digitalwa.statelib.wa.gov/newsite/best.htm
Western States Digital Imaging Best Practices
   www.bcr.org/dps/cdp/best/wsdibp_v1.pdf

References

Alexander, A. and Meehleib, T. (2001). The thesaurus for graphic materials: Its history, use, and future. *Cataloging & Classification Quarterly* 31, 189–212.

Anderson, S., Pringle, M., Eadie, M., Austin, T., Wilson, A., and Polfreman, M. (2006). *Digital images archiving study*, JISC Archiving Study Final Report, Arts and Humanities Data Service. Accessed on October 31, 2009 from: http://ahds.ac.uk/about/projects/archiving-studies/digital-images-archiving-study.pdf.

Ansberry, C. (1989). Alterations of photos raise host of legal, ethical issues. *Wall Street Journal* (January 26), p. B1.

ARL (Association of Research Libraries) (2009). *Special collections in ARL libraries: A discussion report from the ARL Working Group on Special Collections.* Washington, DC: Association of Research Libraries. Accessed on October 31, 2009 from: www.arl.org/bm~doc/scwg-report.pdf.

Armitage, L. H. and Enser, P. G. B. (1997). Analysis of user need in image archives. *Journal of Information Science* 23(4), 287–299.

Arms, C. (1996). Historical collections for the National Digital Library: Lessons and challenges at the Library of Congress. *D-Lib Magazine* (April). Accessed on February 15, 2010 from: www.dlib.org/dlib/april96/loc/04c-arms.html.

Ayris, P. (1998). *Guidance for selecting materials for digitisation.* Joint RLG and NPO Preservation. Accessed on December 20, 2009 from: http://eprints.ucl.ac.uk/492/.

Baca, M. (2002). A picture is worth a thousand words: Metadata for art objects and their visual surrogates. In W. Jones, J. R. Ahronheim, and J. Crawford (Eds.), *Cataloging the web: Metadata, AACR and MARC 21.* (pp 131–138). Lanham, MD: Scarecrow Press.

Baca, M. (2003). Practical issues in applying metadata schemas and controlled vocabularies to cultural heritage information. In S. S. Intner, S. C. Tseng, and M. L. Larsgaard (Eds.), *Electronic cataloguing: AACR2 and metadata for serials and monographs.* (pp. 47–55). Binghamton, NY: Haworth Press.

Baca, M. and Tronzo, W. (2006). Art history and the digital world. *Art Journal* 65(4), 51–55.

Ballard, C. and Teakle, R. (1991). Seizing the light: The appraisal of photographs. *Archives and Manuscripts* 19(1), 43–49.

Barthes, R. (1977). *Image-music-text*. London: Fontana.

Barthes, R. (1981). *Camera lucida: Reflections on photography*. New York: Hill and Wang.

Bartlett, N. (1996). Diplomatics for photographic images: Academic exoticism? *American Archivist* 59(4), 486–494.

Batchen, G. (1990). Burning with desire: The birth and death of photography. *Afterimage* 17(3), 8–11.

Batchen, G. (1999). *Burning with desire: The conception of photography*. Cambridge, MA: MIT Press.

Batchen, G. (2008). *Camera lucida*: Another little history of photography. In R. Kelsey and B. Stimson (Eds.), *The meaning of photography*. (pp. 76–91). New Haven, CT: Yale University Press.

Bate, D. (2001). Blowing it: Digital images and the real. *DPICT* 7, 3–4.

Baxter, G. (2003). The historical photograph: Record, information source, object, resource. *Art Libraries Journal* 28(2), 4–12.

Bearman, D. (1995). Data relationships in the documentation of cultural objects. *Visual Resources* 11, 289–299.

Beaudoin, J. E. (2007). Visual materials and online access: Issues concerning content representation. *Art Documentation* 26(2), 24–28.

Benjamin, W. (1936). The work of art in the age of mechanical reproduction. Accessed on January 1, 2010 from: www.marxists.org/reference/subject/philosophy/works/ge/benjamin.htm.

Bereijo, A. (2004). The conservation and preservation of film and magnetic materials (1): Film materials. *Library Review* 53(6), 323–331.

Berger, J. (1972). *Ways of seeing*. New York: Penguin Books.

Berger, J. and Mohr, J. (1982). *Another way of telling*. New York: Pantheon.

Boles, F. (2005). *Selecting and appraising archives and manuscripts*. Chicago: Society of American Archivists.

Brown, M. W. (1971). The history of photography as art history. *Art Journal* 31(1), 31–36.

Burgin, V. (1982). *Thinking photography*. London: Macmillan.

Burke, P. (2001). *Eyewitnessing: The uses of images as historical evidence*. Picturing history series. Ithaca, NY: Cornell University Press.

Burns, M. (2006). From horse-drawn wagon to hot rod: The University of California's digital image service experience. *Journal of Archival Organization* 4(1/2), 111–139.

Bush, V. (1945). As we may think. *Atlantic Monthly* (July). Accessed on April 20, 2010 from: www.theatlantic.com/magazine/archive/1969/12/as-we-may-think/3881/.

Cawkell, A. E. (1993). Picture-queries and picture databases. *Journal of Information Science* 19(6), 409–423.

Charbonneau, N. (2005). The selection of photographs. *Archivaria* 59, 119–138.

Clarke, G. (1997). *The photograph.* New York: Oxford.

Collins, K. (1998). Providing subject access to images: A study of user queries. *American Archivist* 61: 36–55.

Conway, P. (2000). Overview: Rationale for digitization and preservation. In M. K. Sitts (Ed.), *Handbook for digital projects: A management tool for preservation and access.* (pp. 15–30). Andover, MA: Northeast Document Conservation Center.

Cook, T. (1980). The tyranny of the medium: A comment on "total archives." *Archivaria* 9, 141–149.

Cook, T. (1994). Electronic records, paper minds: The revolution in information management in archives in the post-custodial and post-modernist era. *Archives and Manuscripts* 22(2), 300–328.

Cook, T. (2001). Fashionable nonsense or professional rebirth: Postmodernism and the practice of archives. *Archivaria* 51, 14–35.

Craig, B. (2004). *Archival appraisal: Theory and practice.* Munich: K. G. Saur Verlag.

Crimp, D. (1977). *Pictures.* New York: Committee for the Visual Arts.

Crimp, D. (1995). *On the museum's ruin.* Cambridge, MA: MIT Press.

Daguerre, Louis J. M. (1980). Daguerreotype. In A. Trachtenberg (Ed.), *Classic essays on photography.* New Haven, CT: Leete's Island Books.

Dannenbaum, C. (2008). Seeing the big picture: Integrating visual resources for art libraries. *Art Documentation* 27(1), 13–17.

de Perthuis, K. (2005). The synthetic ideal: The fashion model and photographic manipulation. *Fashion Theory* 9(4), 407–424.

de Polo, A. and Minelli, S. (2006). Digital access to a photographic collection. In L. MacDonald (Ed.), *Digital heritage: Applying digital imaging to cultural heritage.* (pp. 93–114). Oxford: Elsevier.

Deegan, M. and Tanner, S. (2002). *Digital futures: Strategies for the information age.* New York: Neal-Schuman.

Doane, M. (2008). Indexicality and the concept of medium specificity. In R. Kelsey and B. Stimson (Eds.), *The meaning of photography.* (pp. 3–14). New Haven, CT: Yale University Press.

Dooley, J. M. (1995). Processing and cataloging of archival photograph collections. *Visual Resources* 11, 85–101.

Duchein, M. (1983). Theoretical principles and practical problems of *respect des fonds* in archival science. *Archivaria* 16, 64–82.

Dzenko, C. (2009). Analog to digital: The indexical function of photographic images. *Afterimage* 37(2), 19–23.

Elkins, J. (1999). *The domain of images.* Ithaca, NY: Cornell University Press.

Ericson, T. L. (1991). At the "rim of creative dissatisfaction": Archivists and acquisition development. *Archivaria* 33, 66–77.

Ester, M. (1995). Specifics of imaging practice. *Archives & Museum Informatics* 9, 147–185.

Ester, M. (1996). *Digital image collections: Issues and practice.* Washington, DC: Council on Library and Information Resources.

Fawcett, T. (1986). Graphic versus photographic in the nineteenth-century reproduction. *Art History* 9(2), 185–212.

Finnegan, C. A. (2006). What is this a picture of? Some thoughts on images and archives. *Rhetoric & Public Affairs* 9(1), 116–123.

Fontcuberta, J. (2003). Revisiting the histories of photography. In J. Fontcuberta (Ed.), *Photography: Crisis of history.* (pp. 6–17). Barcelona: Actar.

Fraser, M. (1981). Problems presented by photographic collections. *South African Libraries* 48(4), 139–143.

Frey, F. S. and Reilly, J. M. (2006). *Digital imaging for photographic collections: Foundations for technical standards.* Rochester, NY: Image Permanence Institute. Accessed on February 26, 2010 from: www.imagepermanenceinstitute.org/shtml_sub/digibook.pdf.

Fry, E. (2007). From lantern slides to image presentation systems: A discipline in transition. *Indiana Libraries* 26(2), 15–19.

Gernsheim, H. (1977). The 150th anniversary of photography. *History of Photography* 1(1). Accessed on April 15, 2010 from: www.hrc.utexas.edu/exhibitions/permanent/wfp/discovery.html.

Gernsheim, H. (1982). *The origins of photography.* London: Thames & Hudson.

Gernsheim, H. and Gernsheim, A. (1968). *L. J. M. Daguerre: The history of the diorama and the daguerreotype.* New York: Dover.

Goldberg, V. (1991). *The power of photography.* New York: Abbeville.

Goodrum, A. A. (2005). I can't tell you what I want, but I'll know it when I see it: Terminological disconnects in digital image reference. *Reference & User Services Quarterly* 45(1), 46–53.

Green, W. (1989). *Digital image processing.* New York: Van Nostrand Reinhold.

Greene, M. A. (1998). From village smithy to superior vacuum technology: Modern small-records and the collecting repository. *Archival Issues* 23(1), 41–57.

Greene, M. A. and Meissner, D. (2005). More product, less process: Revamping traditional archives processing. *American Archivist* 68(2), 208–263.

Greisdorf, H. F. and O'Connor, B. C. (2008). *Structures of image collections: From Chauvet-Pont-d'Arc to Flickr.* Westport, CT: Libraries Unlimited.

Grundberg, A. (1999). *Crisis of the real: Writings on photography since 1974.* Writers and artists on photography. New York: Aperture.

Gustafson, E. (2005). II. Documents and images: Animating the Institute of Fine Arts lantern slides collection. *Visual Resources Association Bulletin* 32(3), 23–25.

Harris, B. R. (2006). Visual information literacy via visual means: Three heuristics. *Reference Services Review* 34(2), 213–221.

Harvie, C., Martin, G., and Scharf, A. (1970). *Industrialisation and culture 1830–1914.* London: Macmillan.

Hazen, D., Horrell, J., and Merrill-Oldham, J. (1998). *Selecting research collections for digitization.* Washington, DC: Council on Library and Information Resources. Accessed on March 20, 2010 from: www.clir.org/pubs/reports/hazen/pub74.html.

Hedstrom, M. (2000). Descriptive practices for electronic records: Deciding what is essential and imagining what is possible. In R. C. Jimerson (Ed.), *American archival studies: Readings of theory and practice.* (pp. 381–394). Chicago: Society of American Archivists.

Holland, P. (2009). "Sweet it is to scan …": Personal photographs and popular photography. In L. Wells (Ed.), *Photography: A critical introduction.* (pp. 117–165). London: Routledge.

Holmes, O. W. (1859). The stereoscope and the stereograph. *Atlantic Monthly* (June), 738–748, reprinted in Newhall, B. (Ed.) (1980). *Photography, essays and images: Illustrated readings in the history of photography.* New York: Museum of Modern Art.

Holmes, O. W. (1861). Sun-painting and sun-sculpture: With a stereoscopic trip across the Atlantic. *Atlantic Monthly* (August), 13–29.

Homberger, E. (1988). Can we say anything we like about photography? *Word & Image* 4(3/4), 732–778.

Hourihane, C. (2002). It begins with the cataloguer: Subject access to images and the cataloguer's perspective. In M. Baca (Ed.), *Introduction to art image access: Issues, tools, standards, strategies.* Los Angeles: Getty

Research Institute. Accessed on October 17, 2009 from: www.getty. edu/research/conducting_research/standards/intro_aia/hourihane.html.

Howard, R. (2008). Preservation perspectives: Preserving digital information. *Kentucky Libraries*, 72(3), 16–17.

Howe, P. (2001). Photojournalism at a crossroads. *Nieman Reports* 55(3), 25–26.

Hughes, L. (2004). *Digitizing collections: Strategic issues for the information manager*. London: Facet Publishing.

Humphreys, K. (1993). Looking backwards: History, nostalgia, and American photography. *American Literary History* 5(4), 686–699.

Huyda, R. J. (1977). Photographs and archives in Canada. *Archivaria 5*, 3–16.

ICA (International Council on Archives) (2000). *ISAD(G): International standard archival description*. Ottawa: ICA. Accessed on May 7, 2009 from: www.ica.org/sites/default/files/isad_g_2e.pdf.

Ivins, W. M. (1953). *Prints and visual communications*. Cambridge, MA: Harvard University Press.

Jammes, A. and Janis, E. P. (1983). *The art of French calotype, with a critical dictionary of photographers, 1845–1870*. Princeton, NJ: Princeton University Press.

Jones, T. (2001). *An introduction to digital projects for libraries, museums and archives*. Accessed on February 23, 2010 from: http:// images.library.uiuc.edu/resources/introduction.htm.

Kaplan, E. and Mifflin, J. (2000). "Mind and sight": Visual literacy and the archivist. In R. C. Jimerson (Ed.), *American archival studies: Readings in theory and practice*. Chicago: Society of American Archivists.

Keefe, J. M. (1990). The image as document: Descriptive programs at Rensselaer. *Library Trends* 38: 659–681.

Keister, L. H. (1994). User types and queries: Impact on image access systems. In R. Fidel (Ed.), *Challenges in indexing electronic text and images*. (pp. 7–22). Medford, NJ: Learned Information for the American Society of Information Science.

Kenney, A. and Chapman, S. (1996a). Digital conversion of research library materials: A case for full informational capture. *D-Lib Magazine*. Accessed on February 20, 2010 from: www.dlib.org/dlib/ october96/cornell/10chapman.html.

Kenney, A. and Chapman, S. (1996b). *Digital imaging for libraries and archives*. Ithaca, NY: Cornell University Library.

Kenney, A. R. and Rieger, O. Y. (Eds.) (2000). *Moving theory into practice: Digital imaging for libraries and archives*. Mountain View, CA: Research Libraries Group.

Koetzle, H.-M. (2008). *Photo icons: The story behind the pictures 1827–1926*. Los Angeles: Taschen.

Kuny, T. (1998). The digital dark ages? Challenges in the preservation of electronic information. *International Preservation News* 17. Accessed on February 23, 2010 from: http://archive.ifla.org/IV/ifla63/63kuny1.pdf.

Lagoze, C. and Payette, S. (2000). Metadata: Principles, practices, and challenges. In A. R. Kenney and O. Y. Rieger (Eds.), *Moving theory into practice: Digital imaging for libraries and archives*. (pp. 84–100). Mountain View, CA: Research Libraries Group.

Lambert, P. (1977). Photographic documentation and buildings: Relationships past and present. *Archivaria* 5, 60–77.

Layne, S. S. (1994). Some issues in the indexing of images. *Journal of the American Society for Information Science* 45(8), 583–588.

Leary, W. H. (1985). *The archival appraisal of photographs: A RAMP study with guidelines*. Paris: UNESCO. Accessed on November 13, 2009 from: http://unesdoc.unesco.org/images/0006/000637/063749eo.pdf.

Lee, S. D. (2001). *Digital imaging: A practical handbook*. New York: Neal-Schuman.

Library of Congress (2007). Technical standards for digital conversion of text and graphic materials. Accessed on January 11, 2010 from: http://memory.loc.gov/ammem/about/techStandards.pdf.

Lingwood, J. (1986). *Staging the self: Self-portrait photography, 1840–1980s*. London: National Portrait Gallery.

Lipkin, J. (2005). *Photography reborn: Image making in the digital era*. New York: Harry N. Abrams.

Lynch, C. (2002). Digital collections, digital libraries and the digitization of cultural heritage information. *First Monday* (May 5). Accessed on April 16, 2010 from http://131.193.153.231/www/issues/issue7_5/lynch/index.html.

Lytle, A. (2006). Statewide digitization planners conference summary report. *Microform & Imaging Review* 35(1), 19–30.

McCauley, A. (1997). Writing photography's history before Newhall. *History of Photography* 21(2), 87–101.

MacDonald, G. (1980). *Camera: Victorian eyewitness, A history of photography: 1826–1913*. New York: Viking Press.

MacDonald, L. (Ed.) (2006). *Digital heritage: Applying digital imaging to cultural heritage*. Oxford: Elsevier.

McLaughlin, R. B. (1989). The evaluation of historical photographs: Considerations for visual resource curators and librarians in museums and archives. *Art Documentation* 8(2), 55–60.

Mahard, M. (2003). Berenson was right: Why we maintain large collections of historical photographs. *Art Documentation* 22(1), 9–12.

Manovich, L. (2003). The paradoxes of digital photography. In L. Wells (Ed.), *The photography reader*. (pp. 240–249). New York: Routledge.

Marcum, D. (1998). Educating leaders for the digital library. *CLIR Issues* 6. Accessed on March 15, 2010 from: www.clir.org/pubs/issues/issues06.html#educate.

Marien, M. W. (2006). *Photography: A cultural history*. Upper Saddle River, NJ: Pearson Prentice Hall.

Marion, S. L. (2006). Getting beyond? Is photography a lost tradition? *Afterimage* 33(6), 32–36.

Markey, K. (1986). *Subject access to visual resources collections: A model for computer construction of thematic catalogs*. New directions in information management, No. 11. New York: Greenwood Press.

Marsh, Y. (2009). The changing flux in the photograph at the precipice of change: The phototrix and the death of the photograph. *Journal of Media Practice* 10(2/3), 267–272.

Matusiak, K. K. (2006). Information seeking behavior in digital image collections: A cognitive approach. *Journal of Academic Librarianship* 32(5), 479–488.

Melin, W. E. (1986). Photography and the recording process in the age of mechanical reproduction. *Leonardo* 19(1), 53–60.

Mifflin, J. (2007). Visual archives in perspective: Enlarging on historical medical photographs. *American Archivist* 70(1), 32–69.

Miller, J. (2007). The impersonal album: Chronicling life in the digital age. *Afterimage* 35(2), 9–12.

Mitchell, W. (1984). What is an image? *New Literary History* 15(3), 503–537.

Mitchell, W. (2001). *The reconfigured eye: Visual truth in the post-photographic era*. Cambridge, MA: MIT Press.

Moir, M. B. (1993). Finding aids and photographs: A case study in the use of analog optical disc technology to improve access to historical images. *Archivaria* 36, 74–86.

Mora, G. (1998). *Photo speak: A guide to the ideas, movements and techniques of photography, 1839 to the present*. New York: Abbeville Press.

Murphy, J. L. (2003). Link it or lump it: Basic access strategies for digital art representation. *Journal of Library Administration* 39(2/3), 139–160.

Nesmith, T. (1993). Archival studies in English-speaking Canada and the North American rediscovery of provenance. In T. Nesmith (Ed.),

Canadian archival studies and the rediscovery of provenance. (pp. 1–28). Metuchen, NJ: Scarecrow Press.

Nesmith, T. (2006). The concept of societal provenance and records of nineteenth-century Aboriginal–European relations in Western Canada: Implications for archival theory and practice. *Archival Science* 6, 351–360.

Newhall, B. (1964). *The history of photography: From 1839 to the present*. New York: Museum of Modern Art.

NISO (National Information Standards Organization) (2007). *A framework of guidance for building good digital collections.* Accessed on January 15, 2010 from: http://framework.niso.org.

Norris, T. D. (1985). Processing extremely large collections of historical photographs. *Midwestern Archivist* 10(2), 129–134.

O'Toole, J. M. and Cox, R. J. (2006). *Understanding archives and manuscripts.* Archival fundamentals series. Chicago: Society of American Archivists.

Pacey, P. (1983). Information technology and the universal availability of images. *IFLA Journal* 9(3), 230–235.

Panofsky, E. (1937). Style and medium in the moving pictures. *Transition* 26, 121–133.

Panofsky, E. (1939). *Studies in iconology; Humanistic themes in the art of the renaissance.* New York: Oxford University Press.

Pearce-Moses, R. (2005). *A glossary of archival and records terminology.* Chicago: Society of American Archivists. Accessed on May 5, 2009 from: www.archivists.org/glossary/index.asp.

Persinger, T. (2007). Another heyday. *Afterimage* 34(4), 10–11.

Pisciotta, H. (2003). Image delivery and the critical masses. *Journal of Library Administration* 39(2/3), 123–138.

Pitti, D. V. (1999). Encoded archival description: An introduction and overview. *D-Lib Magazine* (November). Accessed on September 6, 2009 from: www.dlib.org/dlib/november99/11pitti.html.

Potonniée, G. (1973). *The history of the discovery of photography.* New York: Arno Press.

Preserving Access to Digital Information (2001). Standards. Accessed on November 15, 2009 from: www.nla.gov.au/padi/topics/43.html.

Pugh, M. J. (2005). *Providing reference services for archives and manuscripts.* Archival fundamentals series. Chicago: Society of American Archivists.

Puglia, S. (1999). The costs of digital imaging projects. *RLG DigiNews* 3(5). Accessed on February 15, 2010 from: http://chnm.gmu.edu/digitalhistory/links/pdf/chapter3/3.10b.pdf.

Ritchen, F. (1999). *In our own image: The coming revolution in photography*. New York: Aperture.

Ritchen, F. (2008). *After photography*. New York: W. W. Norton & Company.

Ritzenthaler, M. and Vogt-O'Connor, D. (2006). *Photographs: Archival care and management*. Chicago: Society of American Archivists.

Ritzenthaler, M., Munhoff, G., and Long, M. (1984). *Archives and manuscripts: Administration of photographic collections*. Chicago: Society of American Archivists.

Rotberg, R. I., and Rabb, T. K. (Eds.) (1988). *Art and history: Images and their meanings*. Cambridge: Cambridge University Press.

Sanders, M., Poynter, P., and Derrick, R. (2000). *The impossible image: Fashion photography in the digital age*. London: Phaidon.

Sandweiss, M. A. (2007). Image and artifact: The photograph as evidence in the digital age. *Journal of American History* (June), 193–202.

Sassoon, J. (1998). Photographic meaning in the age of digital reproduction. *Library & Annotated Science Information Exchange* 29(4), 5–15.

Sassoon, J. (2007). Beyond chip monks and paper tigers: Towards a new culture of archival format specialists. *Archival Science* 7, 133–145.

Schellenberg, T. R. (1965). *The management of archives*. New York: Columbia University Press.

Schlak, T. (2008). Framing photographs, denying archives: The difficulty of focusing on archival photographs. *Archival Science* 8, 85–101.

Schmidle, R. (1996). The smile and promise of digital imaging: Preserving photographs in a digital world. *Library Hi Tech News*, (130), 14–16.

Schwartz, J. M. (1995). "We make our tools and our tools make us": Lessons from photographs from the practice, politics and poetics of diplomatics. *Archivaria* 40, 40–74.

Schwartz, J. M. (2000). "Records of simple truth and precision": Photography, archives, and the illusion of control. *Archivaria* 50, 1–40.

Schwartz, J. M. (2002). Coming to terms with photographs: Descriptive standards, linguistic 'othering,' and the margins of archivy. *Archivaria* 54, 142–171.

Schwartz, J. M. (2004). Negotiating the visual turn: New perspectives on images and archives. *American Archivist* 67(1), 107–122.

Sekula, A. (2003). Reading an archive: Photography between labour and capital. In L. Wells (Ed.), *The photography reader* (pp. 443–452). London: Routledge.

Shapter, M. (2007). Photographs: Whence veracity? *Afterimage* 35(1), 11–17.

Shatford, S. (1984). Describing a picture: A thousand words are seldom cost effective. *Cataloging & Classification Quarterly* 4(4), 13–30.

Shatford, S. (1986). Analyzing the subject of a picture: A theoretical approach. *Cataloging & Classification Quarterly* 6(3), 39–42.

Smith, A. (2002). Strategies for building digitized collections. *Microform & Imaging Review* 31(1), 8–30.

Smith, D. (2003). The surrogate vs. the thing. *Art Documentation* 22(2), 11–15.

Snow, M. (2002). "Visual copy" collections in American institutions. *Art Documentation* 21(2), 4–7.

Sontag, S. (1977). *On photography.* New York: Farrar, Straus and Giroux.

Standage, T. (1998). *The Victorian internet: The remarkable story of the telegraph and the nineteenth century's on-line pioneers.* New York: Walker and Company.

Stiegler, B. (2008). Photography as the medium of reflection. In R. Kelsey and B. Stimson (Eds.), *The meaning of photography.* (pp. 194–197). New Haven, CT: Yale University Press.

Stvilia, B. and Jörgensen, C. (2009). User-generated collection-level metadata in an online photo-sharing system. *Library and Information Science Research* 31, 54–65.

Sutherland, J. (1982). Image collections: Librarians, users, and their needs. *Art Libraries Journal* 7(2), 41–49.

Sutton, S. (2008). Digitizing California history: Issues of selection and description. *Microform & Imaging Review* 37(1), 28–33.

Szarkowski, J. (1966). *The photographer's eye.* New York: Museum of Modern Art.

Szarkowski, J. (1983). Photography and America: Art Institute of Chicago museum studies, Vol. 10. *The Art Institute of Chicago Centennial Lectures,* 236–251.

Tagg, J. (1988). *The burden of representation: Essays on photographies and histories.* London: Macmillan.

Taylor, H. A. (1979). Documentary art and the role of the archivist. *American Archivist* 42(4), 417–428.

Terras, M. M. (2008). *Digital images for the information professional.* Burlington, VT: Ashgate.

Tibbo, H. R. (1993). *Abstracting information retrieval and the humanities: Providing access to historical literature.* Chicago: American Library Association.

Turner, J. M. (1993). Subject access to pictures: Considerations in the surrogation and indexing of visual documents for storage and retrieval. *Visual Resources* 9, 241–271.

Vogt-O'Connor, D. (2006). Appraisal and acquisitions. In M. L. Ritzenthaler and D. Vogt-O'Connor (Eds.), *Photographs: Archival care and management*. (pp. 78–133). Chicago: Society of American Archivists.

Volpe, A. L. (2009). Archival meaning: Materiality, digitization, and the nineteenth-century photograph. *Afterimage* 36(6), 11–16.

Weller, T. and Bawden, D. (2005). The social and technological origins of the information society: An analysis of the crisis of control in England, 1830–1900. *Journal of Documentation* 61(6), 777–802.

Welling, W. (1976). *Collectors' guide to nineteenth-century photographs*. New York: Macmillan.

Wells, L. (2009). On and beyond the white walls: Photography as art. In L. Wells (Ed.), *Photography: A critical introduction*. (pp. 257–310). London: Routledge.

Westney, L. C. (2007). Intrinsic value and the permanent record: The preservation conundrum. *OCLC Systems & Services: International Digital Library Perspectives* 23(1), 5–12.

Wiggins, R. (2001). Digital preservation: Paradox and promise. *Library Journal NetConnect*, Spring, 12–15.

Willis, A. M. (1990). Digitisation and the living death of photography. In P. Hayward (Ed.), *Culture, technology and creativity in the later twentieth century*. (pp. 197–208). Eastleigh, UK: John Libbey.

Wolf, E. M. (2006). When there is no ready-to-wear: Triumphs and failures in creating an image database for interior design. *Art Documentation* 25(1), 25–27.

Woll, J. (2005). User access to digital image collections of cultural heritage materials: The thesaurus as pass-key. *Art Documentation* 24(2), 19–28.

Zinkham, H. (1986). *Descriptive terms for graphic materials*. Washington, DC: Library of Congress.

Zinkham, H. (2006). Description and cataloging. In M. L. Ritzenthaler and D. Vogt-O'Connor (Eds.), *Photographs: Archival care and management*. (pp. 164–206). Chicago: Society of American Archivists.

Index

Breinigsville, PA USA
23 February 2011

256156BV00008B/1/P